NATIONAL INSTITUTE FOR SOCIAL WORK TRAINING SERIES

NO. 14

EDUCATION FOR SOCIAL WORK

READINGS IN SOCIAL WORK

VOLUME IV

Publications by the
National Institute for Social Work Training
Mary Ward House, London, W.C.1

NO. I SOCIAL WORK AND SOCIAL CHANGE
by Eileen Younghusband

NO. 2 INTRODUCTION TO A SOCIAL WORKER
produced by the National Institute for Social Work Training

NO. 3 SOCIAL POLICY AND ADMINISTRATION
by D. V. Donnison, Valerie Chapman and others

NO. 4 SOCIAL WORK WITH FAMILIES
Readings in Social Work, Volume 1
compiled by Eileen Younghusband

NO. 5 PROFESSIONAL EDUCATION FOR SOCIAL WORK IN BRITAIN
by Marjorie J. Smith

NO. 6 NEW DEVELOPMENTS IN CASEWORK
Readings in Social Work, Volume 2
compiled by Eileen Younghusband

NO. 7 THE FIELD TRAINING OF SOCIAL WORKERS
by S. Clement Brown and E. K. Gloyne

NO. 8 DECISION IN CHILD CARE
A Study of Prediction in Fostering Children
by R. A. Parker

NO. 9 ADOPTION POLICY AND PRACTICE
by Iris Goodacre

NO. 10 SUPERVISION IN SOCIAL WORK
by Dorothy E. Pettes

NO. 11 CARING FOR PEOPLE
The 'Williams' Report
on the Staffing of Residential Homes

NO. 12 SOCIAL WORK AND SOCIAL VALUES
Readings in Social Work, Volume 3
compiled by Eileen Younghusband

NO. 13 MOTHER AND BABY HOMES
by Jill Nicholson

EDUCATION FOR SOCIAL WORK

READINGS IN SOCIAL WORK

VOLUME IV

compiled by

EILEEN YOUNGHUSBAND

D.B.E., LL.D.

London

GEORGE ALLEN & UNWIN LTD

RUSKIN HOUSE   MUSEUM STREET

PRINTED IN GREAT BRITAIN
in 11 pt. Fournier Type
BY C. TINLING AND CO. LTD
LIVERPOOL, LONDON AND PRESCOT

PREFACE

This volume is the fourth in a series intended to preserve in more permanent form some of the most valuable articles which have appeared in British and American social work journals in the last few years. There are certain articles which are widely used and quoted, which have indeed become standard works, but are not always easily available to busy social workers. The aim of the present series is thus twofold, both to preserve such articles and make them more widely available, and at the same time by combining together the best that has been written on a given theme by social workers on both sides of the Atlantic to draw attention to recent developments in thought and knowledge.

Although much has been written about the practice of social work, there is very little available on the education and training of social workers. This applies especially to crucial matters like curriculum planning, educational method, principles for the selection of course content, and teaching and learning both in the classroom and field work.

It is surprising when social workers claim, with some justification, to have developed sound educational method in the preparation of practitioners that they should have written little about this. Some of the most useful articles so far available are collected together in the present volume in the hope that they will be valuable not only separately but in combination with each other. They merit careful study and discussion by both schools of social work and field teachers and administrators wherever schools of social work are established.

The National Institute for Social Work Training has received much helpful co-operation from the authors of the articles which form this book and from the journals in which they appeared. In addition to expressing our indebtedness to the authors, the following acknowledgements are made with gratitude to the journals in which the articles originally appeared: *Case Conference* for permission to reprint 'The Place of Scientific Method in Social Work Education'; *International Social Work* for permission to reprint 'Building the Curriculum: The Foundation for Professional Competence'; *Social Casework* for permission to reprint 'The Contribution of Psycho-analysis to Social Work Education', with the permission of the Family Service Association of America, New York; *The Social Service Review* published by the University of Chicago Press, Chicago, Illinois, for permission to reprint 'Teaching Casework by the Discussion Method' (Copyright 1950 by the University of Chicago), 'The Lecture as a Method in Teaching Casework' (Copyright 1951 by the University of Chicago), 'Helping Students in Field Practice Identify and Modify Blocks to Learning' (Copyright 1955 by the University of Chicago), 'A Social Work Approach to Courses in Growth and Behaviour' (Copyright 1960 by the University of Chicago), 'The Place of Help in Supervision' (Copyright 1963 by the University of Chicago), 'The Teacher in Education for Social Work' (Copyright 1968 by the University of Chicago); the United States Department of Health, Education and Welfare, Washington D.C., for permission to reprint 'The Small Group in Learning and Teaching'.

CONTENTS

1

BUILDING THE CURRICULUM: THE FOUNDATION FOR PROFESSIONAL COMPETENCE*

EILEEN BLACKEY

To be concerned with curricula in social work education presupposes that social workers understand and accept the premises which underlie our existence as a profession. We share with other professions certain distinguishing attributes which Ernest Greenwood identifies succinctly as (1) a systematic body of theory; (2) the authority of professional competence; (3) the sanctions bestowed by our communities; (4) a code of ethics and (5) a professional culture.[1] Inherent in these attributes are what Alfred J. Kahn identifies for the social work profession as goals, values, beliefs, apparatus, techniques and the chief method or methods of intervention employed by the professional at a given time.[2] These then are characteristics which provide a fraternity of activity and concern for social workers everywhere, though the operational aspects of this professional framework will and should vary with individual countries.

To bring a subject of this magnitude within manageable bounds, it is essential that we examine and agree upon a number of premises reflecting today's realities which offer us a common frame of reference for undertaking the educational tasks ahead of us.

There are four main points which provide guidance in the examination of curriculum building. The first three are in the nature of assumptions which in my opinion should underlie consideration of the subject. The fourth deals with the subject itself—the curriculum:

1. Social work as an area of professional practice functions within the larger context of the field of social welfare and therefore both its

* Paper given by Dr Eileen Blackey at the 13th International Congress of Schools of Social Work, Washington D.C., August 31–September 3, 1966. Published in *International Social Work*, January, 1967.
    [1] Ernest Greenwood, 'Attributes of a Profession', *Social Work*, New York, Vol. II, No. 3. July 1957.
    [2] Alfred J. Kahn, 'The Function of Social Work', *Issues in American Social Work*, Edited by Alfred J. Kahn, Columbia University Press, 1959.

practice and its education must take cognizance of this broader concern.

2. The development of social work practice, and consequently of social work education, though generally adhering to a universal professional framework, must take place within the political, social, economic and cultural patterns and values of the particular country and must be related to the needs, priorities and resources of that country. In this connection, social work must devise ways of determining these characteristics and conditions as prerequisite to defining the objectives of practice and education in a country.

3. Education for the tasks of social work must take into account the need to prepare for the performance of a range of different functions and for the practice of social work at a number of different levels of responsibility. This in turn requires attention to the development of differentiated training programmes, to the educational levels at which various educational programmes are to be undertaken, and to the educational background of the students who apply.

4. Social work education has by now reached a certain degree of universality in its development of curricula, at the same time that it is expressing a healthy resistance to standardization of curricula around the world. The profession's ability to meet current challenges will depend in no small way on whether social work educators can undertake the formulation of educational programmes in harmony with the previous three assumptions and can acquire the competence and 'know-how' essential to the building of curricula which will achieve the objectives of the profession and remain responsive to change.

The three assumptions need some elaboration in relation to their influence on the building of curricula.

That social work is an integral part of the larger field of social welfare is an assumption which meets with varying degrees of acceptability depending on the country. For many decades, the role of social welfare in the United States was seen as related to what Wilensky and Lebaux call the 'residual' rather than the 'institutional' conception of social welfare. The tendency, Alfred Kahn points out, for social work in the United States to base its practice on 'individual or group adjustive or therapeutic services' strengthened the image of the profession as one concerned primarily if not solely with 'promoting adjustments to, or functioning within, social institutions', thus ignoring, Kahn continues, 'the substantial historical evidence that the nature and specific function of social work (and thus the methods of social workers) must, in fact, reflect the given, changing social situation.'[1] In this latter context,

[1] *Ibid.*

social welfare provisions and programmes are conceived of as an essential and integral part of modern society and as essential to the society's basic institutional arrangements, a point of view which is basic to the goals of social work.

In emerging nations where tradition has not yet taken hold, there is greater recognition of the role of social welfare in national development and more widespread acceptance of social welfare as a permanent institutional structure designed to assist in the rapid changes imposed by political independence, economic growth, industrialization and the break-up of customary patterns and value systems.

Such countries have much to offer to more highly developed, complex societies in which social welfare and social work have too often permitted themselves to be diverted from the mainstream of national, economic and social problems, and the accompanying national and local planning essential to their resolution. In the United States, the most regrettable example of this has been the unwitting disengagement over the past few decades of a large segment of the social work profession from the problems growing out of alienation and powerlessness among the poor and the culturally deprived.

There can be no question in any country of the responsibility which social work has for making itself an effective force in bringing about maximum realization of human and social goals, individually and collectively. This premise dictates that social work education and practice must therefore concern themselves with the processes of social planning and development, with social institutions and their organization, with the positive and negative effects of social change and with the making of social policy, in addition to our professional concern for individuals and their special problems and needs.

The premise that social work practice and education must develop indigenously within a country and in close proximity to its conditions and needs, is not a new one and I am sure there is general agreement as to its validity. What we have not yet succeeded in doing, however, is to effect ways of securing the data and materials on which judgments can be made as to what the nature of social work education *should* be in any one country at a particular time, and of developing professional antennae which will keep us tuned in and responsive to changes occurring in the society so that they may be reflected in on-going curriculum reviews and re-organization.

One of the first steps in the formulation of a curriculum in a school of social work is the development of overall educational goals and specific curriculum objectives for the programme of study. These cannot be arrived at without knowledge and interpretation of the country's history and stage of development, its political, economic, social and cultural trends and problems, its priorities and resources. Such understanding cannot be arrived at by osmosis or trial and error. We must devise conscious and systematic approaches to the acquisition of such insights, through data collection, research findings, personal observation, and any other devices at our command in the countries in which we are conducting our educational programmes.

The knowledge and understanding we seek about a society are of two orders: one, the demographic facts, the known resources, the objective observations; the other, the ideological, philosophical, religious bases of the society, the goals the country has set for itself, the value systems operating within groups and for the country as a whole.

In new nations, this task may be at once more difficult and more possible. More difficult because data collection in a standardized and systematic way usually takes place only after other developmental phases have been experienced. More possible, because in the younger nations, history, events, conditions are all more immediately visible, and may therefore offer more ready clues to what the country needs to do in the selection of priorities, the initiation of social services and the preparation of social workers to staff them.

In longer established societies, it is possible, and I think this is the case in North America, that the knowledge accumulated about a country and its conditions through systematic data collection, research and direct experience can be so massive that those who have responsibility for meeting needs and providing services are confronted with an insurmountable task in delineating and extracting the knowledge, trends and facts which should guide us in an on-going evaluation and re-orientation of our practice and education in social work.

Dr de Jongh has pointed out that we must develop better knowledge of the frequency, character and causation of specific social problems, such as poverty, delinquency, prostitution, alcoholism, etc. and gain through research and other devices better understanding of the effects on human beings of certain rules, institutions and procedures which society has devised to deal with these problems.[1]

In countries which have already reached a higher degree of

---

[1] J. F. de Jongh, 'Schools of Social Work and Social Policy; Old and New Experience', paper presented at International Congress of Schools Social Work, Athens, Greece, 1964. Published in *International Social Work*, January 1965.

sophistication and complexity in their social organization, the task for social work may be one of revitalization and re-orientation, purposefully finding its way back into the mainstream of national, social and economic policy and change. In newly developing societies those responsible for social work education will need to develop blueprints for studying, even with crude instruments, their societal patterns.

If there is one charge which I feel must be given to our profession, it is that those responsible for social work education in all parts of the globe, must submerge themselves in the life of their own societies, must feel viscerally, as well as know intellectually, what the human and social aspirations and needs of their people are; and accept the challenge of working creatively and courageously at devising and inventing approaches which will not only be effective in their own countries but will serve as an inspiration to each of us in our search for solutions.

The social work manpower situation throughout the world requires that we look at more than one route to social work education and that we consider the preparation of social workers at a number of different levels and for a range of different responsibilities. This idea is not a new one. It is reinforced in the literature over and over again, and more particularly in the recent documents prepared by the United Nations.

Any differentiated approach to training must of course be accompanied by a differential approach to the tasks to be performed and to the relationship which exists between and among levels of training and practice. To achieve its purpose, such differentiation must also be related to the deployment of the highly trained and skilled personnel in key places of leadership where their impact on the total social welfare scene can be maximized.

This question of the preparation of social workers differentially for a variety of tasks and at different levels of difficulty is one which is confronting both developing and more developed countries. The ever-increasing shortages in social work personnel demand that the profession begin to differentiate responsibilities and tasks which can be performed by people with different types and levels of training. This is a task in which the experiences of developing countries can contribute new insights and point new directions for all countries.

The building of curricula in social work education should consist of a set of systematic and disciplined processes. What is frequently ignored is the fact that these processes require specific knowledge and skills on the part of those responsible for curriculum building if curricula are to be developed and executed effectively. It is important, therefore, that provision be made by the profession to enable educators to become proficient in this activity.

To screen from an increasingly expanding literature on curriculum building in social work that which can suitably fit within the confines of this article is an exceedingly difficult thing to do without making the material seem fragmented and disjointed. Reduced to its simplest terms, it is the 'why', 'what' and 'how' of social work training with which we are concerned and I shall try to develop my ideas within this general framework.

The 'why, what and how' frame of reference which supports social work as a profession, and thereby guides both its practice and education, has been identified as consisting of social work values, social work functions and social work methodology. While there may be universal acceptance of the structural utility of such a professional framework, there is also recognition of the cultural variations which will determine the emphases and implementation of it in individual countries. In this context, it is more accurate to think in terms of 'curricula' than 'the curriculum'.

Nevertheless, the profession cannot be practised nor taught without reference to its constituent parts and their relationship one to the other. Our methods of social work intervention, for example, must grow out of our values and functions. Professional functions must flow from values (the society's as well as the profession's), and in turn serve as one of the determinants in the nature of services to be provided and the choice of methods of intervention to be adopted. And undergirding the total professional framework are the values of social work.

Coming to agreement on the values held by the profession is not an easy matter, particularly when they are viewed within a cross-cultural context. Allowing for these differences, however, it is generally agreed that the profession is concerned with two sets of values, each of a different order. One set is people-oriented, the other society-oriented. Our people-oriented values support belief in and concern for (1) the worth, dignity and well-being of the individual, and (2) the integrity and well-being of the group, meaning individuals, family, small groups, and communities, including the world community. The society-oriented values are concerned with (1) progress in economic development towards the realization of more resources for people and (2) the value placed on security in the physical, economic and social spheres as basic to human progress and fulfilment.

The implications of these values for curriculum building are far reaching. They permeate and guide the nature and scope of the content of the curriculum and re-inforce the assumptions that social work is a part of and must be concerned with the broader field of social welfare, and must relate itself to the values of the society in which it exists.

The functions of the profession have generally been historically responsive to societal needs and conditions as they exist in individual countries around the world. Dependent on these needs and conditions, social work functions, as they get translated into services, may encompass a limited or broad range of activities, may emphasize some functions to the exclusion of others at any one time, or may actually be malfunctioning in relation to what the needs and conditions demand.

Social work has experienced considerable shifts over the years in what it conceives of as its functions. In general, there would be agreement on the curative and restorative functions carried by social work, spanning activities from the meeting of mass need to the deployment of all available resources on behalf of the rehabilitation of an individual, family or group. However, today, in addition to these important functions, attention is sharply focused on social work's role in prevention and social planning. And in connection with these two latter functions, social work has begun to develop its knowledge and practice competence towards more active identification of gaps in services to people, organization of communities towards the provision of services, identification of the impact of social institutions and systems on people and the sharpening of our knowledge and skills in bringing about social change.

What social work sees as its functions at any one point in a country's development, and what the country itself sees as priorities, will directly affect the emphasis social work education will give to preparing social workers for the social services. At the same time, social work education has a responsibility for anticipating the next steps in a country's development so as to equip graduates to take a lead in the initiation of services directed towards the meeting of human and social needs at higher levels of realization and social functioning when they can be achieved.

Regardless of the stage of development in a particular society, students should be taught that the functions of social work encompass and permit of a range of activities which may in succession, or simultaneously, give attention to problems requiring curative or restorative treatment; to the preventive aspects of problems; to social reform and to social planning and social policy.

B

In its development, the methodology of social work has tended to follow the constituencies defined by the profession as individuals, groups and communities, resulting in the formulation of the social work methods, developed almost exclusively by American social work, of social casework, social group work and community organization. Although methodology should flow logically from function and should constitute flexible professional tools for the carrying out of services, we have tended in too many countries to permit methods to become an end in themselves. The most dramatic evidence of this is the extent to which the three social work methods, but more especially American casework, have been utilized by other countries with little relationship to their suitability for the local conditions and needs. Equally dramatic and unfortunate is the extent to which American social work has become 'methods-bound'.

Since professional education in social work in North America grew indirectly out of practice and conducted its preparation of practitioners through apprenticeship programmes in its early years, it is understandable that the United States developed a long and strong commitment to what Harriett Bartlett terms the 'skill' method of practice. With this came the intensification of specialized practice skills and the emergence of the now famous American trilogy of casework, group work and community organization.

For reasons which could themselves constitute a paper, American social work now finds itself possessed by rather than being the designer of its methods of providing services. At a time when social work must be creatively and quickly responsive to the phenomenal social changes going on around us, and the strategies of social work intervention must be flexibly applied in meeting problems, we find only too often that the delivery of social services is straight-jacketed by the 'skills' model of social casework, with its built-in sub-culture of the 'one-to-one' relationship, the office interview, a middle class outlook, and screening in favour of the 'motivated' client.

In North America, social group work and community organization have not had as long a history as casework, nor have they been as widespread in application, but the same observation may in time be made of them if we continue to allow agencies to be structured as casework agencies, group work agencies or community organization agencies and in turn, the services offered to be dictated by the method of practice rather than by the client's problem and his 'life-space' needs.

Not only American social workers but our colleagues in other countries need to examine closely the phenomenon which we have permitted to develop whereby the organizational structure of an agency and the social work methods established to implement that service have become institutionalized to the point where our practice and our education tend to be governed by the method of practice rather than by the problem requiring solution. The methods of casework, group work and community organization have been established as gospel in many places so we tend to adopt them because they exist rather than creating approaches and ways of helping which would be best suited to the problems and conditions confronting those seeking help.

In this connection, Dr Pusie reminds us that specialized training for social work was first developed in countries with a pronounced individualistic outlook on social problems and a corresponding understanding of social welfare services as a means of helping in the process of individual change and adjustment. Pusic adds that even though these countries have themselves progressed beyond this stage of thinking towards awareness of other dimensions of social problems, past attitudes have been preserved, sometimes unconsciously, in the training programmes. Furthermore, these are often transmitted to developing countries as models of social work practice and education to be adopted.[1] The educational task lies in the selection, modification and re-orientation of these contributions in such a way that they advance rather than divert or block the programmes needed in our respective countries.

The profession's framework of values, functions and methods is transmitted through what we have come to call the 'knowledge, attitudes and skills' base of the curriculum. Though conveniently brief, this description no longer reflects accurately what we are trying to do. For one thing, 'knowledge' has taken on many dimensions, including major contributions from other disciplines as well as a rapidly growing body of theory of our own. 'Attitudes' are derived from 'values' but the term falls short of conveying the force of the impact which this component of the profession's culture has on its students in today's world. The term 'skills' is reminiscent of an apprenticeship era. We are more concerned today with 'professional competence' as defined by the nature of the task to be learned and the level of responsibility to be carried. It is also true that knowledge and competence are identifiable through specific curriculum content in courses and field instruction, values or attitudes are not so readily

[1] *Reappraisal of the United Nations Social Service Programme*. Submitted by Dr Eugen Pusic. Social Commission *ad hoc* Working Group on Social Welfare, United Nations, February 5, 1965. (E/CN.5/AC.12/L.3/add.1).

identified—rather, they permeate the entire exposure to learning which the student undergoes.

In the formulation of a social work curriculum, determination of the areas of knowledge to be included is an intricate task, but we are moving closer to the delineation of what constitutes a core programme of study specific to our profession. The *Third International Survey on Training for Social Work*, published by the United Nations in 1958,[1] represented our first common effort to identify the knowledge areas essential to social work training. These were described then as (1) the study of man; (2) the study of society; (3) social work theory and method; and (4) field instruction. Today, we are dealing essentially with the same general components in professional education but we have done much to sharpen and refine the interrelatedness of these components and to identify more clearly what constitutes the theoretical base of social work knowledge and method.

In the major knowledge areas of the understanding of man and society and their interaction one with another, undoubtedly the most forceful contributions that have been made in recent years have come from the advancing theories of the biological and social sciences. As a result of these advances we are much closer to viewing man and his social environment as a physiological, psychological and social entity and the conditions of health and illness, normalcy and deviation, as part of a continuum in human functioning.

An ever increasing volume of new knowledge about man and society is at our disposal. The task of social work education lies in becoming sufficiently familiar with it to discern what concepts and other content are appropriate for application to social work. This in turn assumes that we know to what use we wish to put such knowledge. The development of theory by any field of endeavour is directed towards its use in the context of the particular problems and research of that field and cannot therefore be lifted bodily out of that context and made to explain problems and offer solutions in an entirely different field, even though related. The utilization of theoretical contributions from other fields of knowledge by social work necessitates (1) selectivity with regard to what knowledge has utility for social work. In other words, we must approach other disciplines with our own practice questions in mind, and (2) a process of reformulation and synthesis which organizes such knowledge into a conceptual framework with specific applicability to the tasks of social work.

[1] *Training for Social Work, Third International Survey*, United Nations, New York, 1958.

Since the vast majority of schools of social work in the world offer curricula which are either a part of undergraduate education in academic institutions or are independent schools offering programmes on a par with undergraduate education, one of the major educational problems to be overcome in developing a curriculum is that of maintaining an appropriate balance between subjects which give students a broad general knowledge and those which are more specifically in the area of professional education.

In this connection, the length of time available for the programme of study will be a significant factor in determining the selection and arrangement of courses. If a programme of study at the undergraduate level is two or three years in length, it stands to reason the task will be more difficult than if the programme is four years in duration.

If it is at all possible, it is more productive for the students' learning if the background courses in the social sciences can be developed with particular reference to social problems, their causation, nature and prevention. The educational objectives of the building of this aspect of the curriculum, therefore, should be (1) that the students should acquire in a systematic manner an appreciation of the broad theoretical contribution of the particular field to an understanding of man and society; and (2) that major concepts from the particular field which have relevance for social work will be adequately treated as a basis for the courses in social work which follow.[1]

The expectations of students who come into social work are directed towards an early identification with the profession they have chosen. It is therefore important in their first year of study, even though it may be heavily weighted with background courses, that some courses be offered which will spark the student's interest and increase his motivation towards social work. Often this can be accomplished by including an introductory course on social welfare and by building in opportunities for community studies and field observations. Identification with the profession is also enhanced if the social work faculty has a responsibility for teaching such a course and for guiding the field activity.

The knowledge which social work draws from the biological, behavioural and social sciences represents only one major segment of our curriculum-building task.

There is no question that the profession of social work is now embarked on a knowledge-building course, and is engaged in the

[1] Eileen Blackey, 'The Development of the Social Work Curriculum in Israel', *International Social Work*, Vol. V, No. 2., April, 1962.

processes of evolving, testing and formulating knowledge and theory which should more and more constitute the basis of our education and practice. We are constructing our knowledge through a number of different routes: increased engagement in research; more sophisticated use of our 'practice-wisdom'; selection and translation of contributions from other fields; and the application of an increasingly effective set of educational tools to the tasks of curriculum building.

In the reappraisal of the United Nations social service training programmes, Pusic notes that there is a subtle change going on in the understanding of the content and meaning of training in the various countries. There is, for example, less dogmatism with regard to the curricula prescribed or the methods of teaching employed while greater store is set by the versatility and essential flexibility of the training method provided. Pusic contends that the whole question of training has to be radically re-thought, a greater variety of variables and possibilities taken into account and new forms of training developed corresponding to new welfare services in social situations which really have no precedent.[1] While Pusic is applying this last point to developing societies, I would underscore its applicability to rapidly changing industrialized societies as well.

If we accept these observations as valid, our approach to curriculum building must take into account that at most any guide posts should suggest the broad areas which guide our selection and emphasis in curriculum content and some systematic processes by which a curriculum actually comes into being. Within these general outlines, the responsibility for the development of purpose, direction, and emphasis in curricula must rest with individual schools and countries. It is in this spirit that the following comments are made.

The curriculum content which is becoming increasingly identifiable as particular to the profession of social work takes the form of a number of interlocking clusters of subject areas, namely, (1) content which is concerned with human behaviour within the context of the social functioning of people as individuals, and as members of small groups or larger communities; (2) content which is concerned with social welfare in all its major aspects—its philosophy, organization, policy, programmes, planning and evaluation; (3) content which is concerned with the methods of intervention utilized by social work in dealing with problems or needs presented by individuals, groups or communities; (4) content concerned with social research, including the utilization of existing research findings in our teaching and the

[1] *Ibid.*

preparation of students in the rudiments of research methodology, together with opportunities to apply this knowledge in the exploration of some aspects of a social problem no matter how small. And finally, (5) the laboratory aspect of the curriculum provided through the field instruction activity which hopefully offers students opportunity to test out and learn from any and all of the content areas around which their course work is organized. The day should be past when we view field instruction as related only to the social work methods courses in the curriculum. Students should have the maximum possible opportunity in their field activity to put to use the knowledge, concepts and principles which the other content areas of the curriculum are designed to teach. This is said with full recognition of the difficult educational task this presents in the preparation of field teachers to become sufficiently knowledgeable about the curriculum to be able to carry such an integrative responsibility. It is easier to achieve a goal, however, if one is convinced of its importance.

Because the development of field instruction facilities and also the determination of the content of field learning present such a universal dilemma, it seems appropriate to pursue this point somewhat further. In field instruction as in social work methods, we have, over the decades, permitted certain approaches and traditional ways of doing things to cement field instruction into a mould which we are now finding it difficult to crack. It should be noted, however, that exciting and creative attempts are being made in some countries to bring to field instruction the same freshness and flexibility which we are attempting to bring to the teaching of theoretical material in the social work methods. This is a logical development since field instruction must be an expression of the philosophy and content of the total academic curriculum.

Recognizing that the availability of a sufficient number of social agency programmes of a quality desirable for the teaching of students constitutes a real problem for most countries, the responsibility then must rest with those in social work education to design learning experiences for students that are innovative and imaginative in the sense of utilizing whatever resources are available even though they may not be of a highly developed order. This may involve more field teaching by school faculty and/or training programmes for field teachers who are on agency staffs. It is the educational use and control of such resources that constitutes the core of our responsibility, in this area as well as in other areas of curriculum building.

Perhaps the most difficult of all is to develop curricula which will prepare graduates to meet effectively the demands of present day practice yet at the same time provide them with the professional equipment to move with the changing times and to remain alert and responsive to events and trends in human and societal endeavour.

The knowledge explosion in all fields makes it mandatory that we should teach students how to go on learning rather than teaching them only the technique of the moment. Jerome S. Bruner in his book *The Process of Education* asks how exposure to learning can be made to count in the students' thinking for the rest of their lives, and goes on to say that the answer to this question lies in giving students an understanding of the fundamental structure of whatever subjects are taught.[1] To the extent to which we can teach the interrelatedness of ideas as they bear on a problem, rather than simply the mastery of facts and techniques, to that degree will we be helping students to see the transferability of their knowledge to a range and variety of situations now and in the future.

In this realm as in others, however, we are confronted with the variations in countries in relation to stages of development in educational systems and philosophies. The educational task of social work educators whose students have come up through the route of 'rote learning' in their previous education can be a very discouraging one indeed. One is faced not only with the task of social work education but actually with the responsibility for correctional education directed towards enabling students to think for themselves, to experience the sharing of ideas with others and to develop an ability to grasp abstract ideas and regroup them for use in other contexts.

It must be accepted and appreciated that achievement related to such goals has a relative quality. Schools must set their expectations within realizable bounds and educators must deal realistically with the constraints which may be present in their particular situations. It is well to recognize though that the process of education cannot be separated from the content of education and that in our efforts to become more knowledgeable and skilful in curriculum building, we must include both.

I have elected to end rather than begin the paper with what might be considered guiding principles in curriculum building. Social work education's indebtedness to Dr Ralph W. Tyler[2] in this area is great indeed. The simplicity of his frame of reference for approaching

---

[1] Jerome S. Bruner, *The Process of Education*, Harvard University Press, 1963, p. 11.
[2] *Building the Social Work Curriculum*, Report of the National Curriculum Workshop, Allerton, Illinois, June 13–18, 1960. Council on Social Work Education, New York.

curriculum building might leave us somewhat abashed that we had not arrived at it earlier from our own deliberations and experience, except for the fact that as one looks behind the simplicity of phrase one recognizes a complexity and sophistication of ideas and tasks that command all our resources and skills. The tasks encountered in curriculum building are grouped by Tyler under four main headings: objectives, learning experiences, organization and evaluation.

To say that the development of the purposes and objectives of the overall curriculum, as well as those of each of its component parts, is the cardinal principle and first step in curriculum building may seem obvious, even trite. Yet this is the major guiding task to all others. It lays the foundation for the school's relationship to the society in which it exists, for the characteristics of the student body to be admitted, for the nature of the curriculum to be developed and for the type of graduate to be produced.

The selection and definition of learning experiences best suited to enabling students to attain the educational objectives, the second step defined by Tyler, refers to the expectations imposed by the curriculum with regard to what the student will be expected to learn. Tyler defines these objectives in terms of (1) the behavioural aspect and (2) the content aspect. What are the ways of thinking, feeling, and acting that the student needs to learn to become a social worker? What knowledge content will the student be expected to understand? These two aspects, the content and the behavioural, are so closely related that they must be defined almost as one process in achieving this step in developing the curriculum.[1]

The organization of learning experiences into courses and programmes is the logical third step in this process, and much more easily said than accomplished. This step demands the ultimate in faculty collaboration and adherence to what Tyler calls the working principles of continuity, progression and integration in the formulation of courses, horizontally and vertically, in the programme. Continuity provides for continuing emphasis over a period of time on the major learning expected of the student, the reinforcement in a variety of learning experiences of the major concepts and behaviours required by the curriculum. Sequence in a curriculum involves planning so that each learning experience will add something new to previous experiences but enable the student to go beyond them. Integration refers to perceiving connections, either likenesses or differences, with what one has already acquired, thus accelerating and extending learning.

[1] *Ibid.*

While the student himself must work at this integrative task, the curriculum must also aid him through facilitating the integration.[1]

Tyler's fourth step in this framework of principles is that of devising methods for judging the effectiveness of the curriculum through evaluation of the learning achieved by the students. This may be accomplished in some measure by the results of examinations and by observations of the success of graduates in the field. Formal student reactions to their programme, solicited through structured questionnaires can also be helpful in assessing the programme of study. Of course, a permanent curriculum policy committee in the school ensures an on-going examination of curriculum trends and problems and keeps the faculty alert to problems of overlapping course content, gaps in knowledge areas, the educational tasks connected with the 'reinforcement' rather than the 'repetition' of the concepts taught and so on.

Any framework of principles in social work education can come to fruition only if it utilizes the yeast with which this article has been dealing. By itself, it has no meaning.

In closing, I should like to summarize several crucial obligations which I think lie ahead of us in this important undertaking of social work education.

Firstly, there are many tasks in social work education which we are not yet equipped to undertake but for which we must prepare ourselves. One of these is the arduous task of building curriculum content and field learning in the areas of social planning and community development, social policy and social change. These are extremely abstract concepts and if taught as such without the designing of models which will enable students to put the concepts to use, social workers will be no closer to effective involvement in these processes in the future than they are now in many countries. Schools in individual countries should be able to document empirically what is now going on in relation to these processes, but the distillation of the principles and the organization of units of knowledge can best be undertaken by working groups, including educators and practitioners, on a regional or country-wide basis.

A second responsibility of crucial importance is the need to continue the refinement and delineation of social work tasks with a view to preparing curricula for different types and levels of social work personnel. Until we tackle this problem with determination and vision, there remains a certain futility in our efforts to make social work education truly an effective force in social change.

[1] *Ibid.*

A third important undertaking must be that of making adequate provision for the development of faculties with reference to their responsibilities as curricula builders. The educational tasks to be undertaken truly require special knowledge and skill and teachers should no more be expected to be proficient in them without formal preparation than we could expect students to emerge as professional practitioners without designated preparation. This is an objective in which international resources as well as those available in individual countries or regions, should be put in use, and soon.

The last and most comprehensive task is that of developing a flexible master plan to assist social work education, and practice, to keep on the course and to prevent some of the hardening of the arteries to which we are sometimes susceptible. Though somewhat global in scope, there are four logical and sequential steps which should prove to be an effective compass.

The first step is a diagnostic one, that of determining the nature of the human and social problems with which the profession, at any one place and time, must concern itself, the nature of the societal environment in which the problems exist and the values and goals which are operating within the society and the profession. The second phase leads us to a definition of the specific social work tasks which should be performed within such a diagnostic framework in order to accomplish the problem-solving goals. The third step requires decision as to what institutional provisions should be developed that will be compatible with the goals, and only then would we move to the last step of determining the processes or methods by which the tasks are to be translated into services to people, whether as individuals or in groups and communities. In such a frame of reference, the methods of social work become a means to an end rather than an end in themselves.

The social work curriculum is without doubt one of the foundations for professional competence but professional competence is after all a relative thing. As social work educators we are dedicated to its realization, but it will be and should be arrived at in various parts of the world in different ways, at different paces and through different routes. It will be these differences which will provide the vitality that professional education must have for the fulfilment of our social responsibility and the contemporary roles of our profession.

2

THE SMALL GROUP IN LEARNING
AND TEACHING*

MARY LOUISE SOMERS

In a slim little volume of philosophical essays, with the altogether intriguing title *On Knowing—Essays for the Left Hand*,[1] Jerome S. Bruner writes of a highly productive, creatively inventive small group of which he was a member for a period of a year. He writes of his own experience as a member of that group, describing it as an 'illuminating' one, in which he discovered that although he had no technical knowledge about the particular task of the group, he was able to come up with some respectable ideas and even to invent a device which was helpful in the task. He points up how his own creativity was increased through his participation in that group, and comments that 'the effectiveness of the group members consisted in their sense of freedom to explore possibilities, in their devotion to elegant solutions, and in the interplay among them that, in effect, made each man stronger in the group than individually.'[2]

There have been times, perhaps, when others of us have known within ourselves this increased and enhanced creativity beyond our usual, because of our participation in a group which was especially meaningful to us—when 'the sense of freedom to explore possibilities, the devotion to elegant solutions, and the interplay among the members' strengthened each and all of us.

We have known, too, the deep frustration, the irritations, the diminished sense of self that result from participation in a group whose members may labour long but whose major production may be rather shabby, forlorn ideas and a mighty accumulation of hostilities, anger at self and others, and a determination never to become involved again.

Thus our own experience tells us that groups have potentials for affecting our thinking, feeling, and acting, even to the point of

* Published in 'Learning and Teaching in Public Welfare', Report of the Co-operative Project on Public Welfare Staff Training, Vol. I, U.S. Department of Health, Education and Welfare, Washington D.C., November, 1963.
[1] Jerome S. Bruner, *On Knowing – Essays for the Left Hand*, The Belknap Press of Harvard University Press, Cambridge, Massachusetts, 1962, p. 11.
[2] *Ibid.*

strengthening or diminishing our individual selves and self concepts, as well as our social functioning in many life situations. My own professional concerns of social work practice and of professional education for social work have been and are imbedded in the use of small groups for social work treatment and the use of small groups as one means of learning and teaching a professional practice.

We often make an underlying assumption which should be stated— that is, we assume that the task of an educational group is individual learning, and that we wish to explore not whether this is true, but how this fact or truth may be implemented. We have given up, and I hope for good, the need to posit or create an artificial dichotomy between the individual and the group. Groups are comprised of individuals, and it is dangerous as well as unrealistic and unproductive to assume that groups as groups are always compatible with or never compatible with the interests, needs, concerns, growth and development of individuals. Rather, it is much more reasonable and of consequence to ask about, to search for, to identify the factors in groups (in our instance, groups with educational purpose and task) which seem to enhance the learning and creativity of individuals, and the factors which seem to diminish or to tend to destroy the learning and creativity of individuals. For this first major task of this paper, I shall draw upon knowledge derived from small group research and theory, screen it through the lens of the educational task, select some content from the behavioural sciences, especially that segment dealing with small groups, and try to suggest some findings which can help us to know and to understand the nature of the structure and functioning of small groups, especially of those having an educational purpose or task to perform.

But this is only one part of the learning-teaching transaction. The second major attempt of this paper is to identify (from experience, and from the developing body of what might be termed 'social practice theory') basic principles of ways of working with small groups of learners in order to facilitate learning and to increase or enhance creativity. In this second aspect of the paper the understanding and use of the small group for educational diagnosis and for teaching process will be developed.

The essential considerations come down to this: if we believe that the major and appropriate task of the educational group is individual learning, how can the learners in interaction with each other and with the teacher, who is in interaction with each learner, and with the group as an entity, together meet the demands and expectations of the learning-teaching transaction and 'contract'? I hope these questions are not trivial, nor on the other hand, impossibly difficult. It is my intent to pose middle-range questions, the questions which dwell, in a sense, in that middle ground of collaborative work among the behavioural scientists and the social practitioners, the middle ground of Ernest Greenwood's 'applied-oriented scientist and theory-oriented practitioner',[1] the fertile ground which carries the roots of the idea that a theory which cannot be applied is a questionable theory. This is the ground not only for acquiring knowledge (in our acquisitive society) but also for advancing knowledge by means of diffusion and application. There are, thus, two major foci—the small group in learning and the small group in teaching. Each will be explored and then, in a sense, we shall again put together what we have separated temporarily for sake of analysis.

But before these foci can be explored through the major questions relevant to each, we need a theoretical framework dealing with small groups and with learning as change. I shall attempt to sketch very briefly some essential ingredients of our current knowledge about small groups, their structure and dynamics, and shall apply these concepts, definitions and propositions to small groups formed for educational purposes. I shall also comment briefly on learning as change, and on the nature of changes which small groups seem able to facilitate. Education implies behavioural changes in individuals—changes in thinking, feeling and doing—and therefore some propositions about the nature and consequences of such changes in individuals, as facilitated within and through small groups, are also essential ingredients with which to work.

We know from our own experience, and research has confirmed our experiential knowledge, that throughout the life span of individuals in our democracy, various groups experiences reflect in essence the interdependence between the individual and his society. It is in the small group that the individual and society confront each other at close range, for better or for worse, in their interrelatedness. All small groups, the family, the neighbourhood play group, peer group associations of various kinds, or educational, work and avocational groups of a great range and variety, have inherent within them the very essence of the support and demand, the give and take, the getting and giving, the benefits and the expectations which characterize the

¹ Ernest Greenwood, 'The Practice of Science and the Science of Practice', *The Planning of Change*, ed. by Warren G. Bennis, Kenneth D. Benne, Robert Chin; Holt, Rinehart and Winston, New York, 1961, p. 81.

individual's relationship to society throughout his life. The importance of the small group in maintaining the integrity of the individual and the integrity of society is now well known and established.

We know, too, by now that it is unrealistic to try to forge a dichotomy between the individual and the group. Whatever is intra-personal (operating within the personality of the individual learner) is operating interpersonally in his relationships with others. We know, too, that in every small group, including those formed for educational purposes, there are structure, process and content, each of which is related to the others. Each must be understood and utilized by the teacher if he is to make effective use of the group in achieving educational objectives. Another way of putting this is to say that every small group works on tasks and works on relationships—the teacher must also relate to and deal effectively with the group in both of these major dimensions of group life and functioning.

It is true of all small groups, but especially clear and notable in those formed for educational purposes, that the crucial ambiguity is that of dependence—interdependence. This is particularly a prevalent concern and must be constantly dealt with in the educational group, since dependence conflicts relative to the authority of the teacher may be exacerbated as well as modified in the small group. The dependence conflict may be affected by the inter-dependence relationships. The continuing conflicts of inter-dependence which may show in rivalries, competitive interaction for place among peers, and the more or less open expression of aggression and of hostility surrounding both authority and peer figures may sap the problem-solving strength of individuals and group and diminish or sidetrack the learning of individuals if major emotional investment must go into these conflicts for extensive periods of time.

I have been using the concept of 'small group' without specifying any number or being definitive about size. There is no magic number, widely accepted as the 'proper' number for a small group. But many social scientists these days would agree that two to twenty-five persons might be within a group appropriately termed 'small'. Experience has often seemed to tell us the same thing. I have heard many experienced teachers of adults say that if a class is larger than 25, a great deal is lost, especially if the teacher wishes to utilize the discussion method of teaching as the major method of instruction. Comments will ordinarily follow concerning 'about 15 as an ideal number', enough to offer richness to each other and to keep the discussion flowing and interesting.

Experience also tells us and research has confirmed that most individuals find it impossible to sustain direct relationships with any more than ten or eleven others at a time; when a small group reaches twelve in number, it seems inevitably to break into sub-groups. Thus in groups composed of twelve or more, individuals seem to find it necessary to relate to the larger structure through closer attachment to a sub-group structure as a kind of interstitial layer. Sub-groups which enable individuals to feel comfortable within them, and which are positively related to the group goals can thus sustain and facilitate individual and group goal achievement. If such sub-structures are against the group goal, they can very effectively diminish individual participation and impede or even prevent progress towards the group goal.

A teacher who makes an attempt to understand and to take into account the structure and dynamics of the group in order to facilitate the learning-teaching process, must necessarily be able to formulate a diagnostic assessment at two levels—individual and group. In the group formed for educational purposes, the teacher must be able to formulate an educational diagnosis of each individual and to continue to revise that educational diagnosis as the evidence of the individual's response to the learning-teaching situation becomes clear. But if the teacher is to utilize knowledge and understanding of the group for purposes of furthering individual educational diagnosis and of further-ing the learning-teaching processes, then a group diagnosis is also essential. In order to formulate an intelligent, meaningful and useful group diagnosis, the teacher must have a relevant set of concepts by means of which to think about and to assess group structure and functioning. There are many such sets of concepts, and one of the difficult and frustrating facts of life for social practitioners (such as social workers and teachers) is that the various sets of small group concepts developed by the behavioural scientists are not yet congruent with each other—the same concept may be called by different names, and the same name may be used to denote different phenomena or processes. However, the picture is not nearly so discouraging as it was even ten years ago. A number of social scientists are devoting their professional lifetimes to sorting, defining, clarifying, pinning down these elusive notions, and we shall one day have a more well defined, agreed upon set of concepts for use in group diagnosis. Meanwhile, in my estimation, as teachers of social work practitioners, we have two most helpful sources upon which to draw: the set of small group concepts as formulated originally by Dr Grace Coyle of Western Reserve University and as explicated and applied by Dr Eileen

Blackey in reference to staff training.[1] These formulations and applications bear concentrated study, working through and testing in teaching.

Thus it is that the teacher, in formulating an individual educational diagnosis, must assess as one aspect of this diagnosis, how each individual learner is or is not utilizing the educational group in efforts to meet his own educational goals and the expectations of the teacher. The teacher must also be able to assess the nature and functioning of the educational group as a group, using for his assessment such concepts as group structure, individual and group goals, inter-personal relations, group controls, group problem-solving, group cohesion and morale, and group norms. In a sense, the teacher formulates what I term an on-going, running or dynamic educational diagnosis of each individual and of the group, of the development and changes characterizing both, and a running diagnosis of the relationship of each individual learner to the group and the learning consequences and outcomes of both educational content and of the inter-action. Since the task of an educational group is individual learning, this continuous diagnostic assessment of individual and group and the continuous revision of these assessments in the light of evaluation of progress towards educational goals are essential to effective learning and teaching.

This leads into the second basic ingredient in the theoretical framework—the nature of changes to be sought through the educational process and the relationship of the small group to these changes. For this sketch, I am drawing heavily on two sources—some of the current change theory developed in recent behavioural science formulations,[2] and Dr Ralph Tyler's educational formulations.[3]

As social workers we know that human beings actively and with great strength resist the very changes which they say they wish to bring about in themselves and in society. We find these same tendencies in ourselves, and we find that the ambivalent wanting and not wanting is a very important feature of all learning. All of us want to have already learned, and resist going through the changes involved in learning.

[1] For detailed description and explanation of these concepts, both in basic theory and in application, see Grace L. Coyle and Margaret Hartford, *Social Process in the Community and Group*, Council on Social Work Education, New York, 1958 and Eileen A. Blackey, *Group Leadership in Staff Training*, U.S. Department of Health, Education, and Welfare, Washington, D.C., 1957.

[2] See 'Selected Examples of the Influence Process', in *The Planning of Change*, eds. Warren Bennis, Kenneth Benne, Robert Chin, Holt, Rinehart and Winston, New York, 1961, pp. 559–615.

[3] Ralph W. Tyler, *Basic Principles of Curriculum and Instruction*, The University of Chicago Press, Chicago, Illinois, 1950, *passim*.

C

When we examine the major themes which appear in the current contributions of social science to a theory of change in human beings, we find several propositions which occur again and again:[1] (1) Some feelings of failure and loss are always involved in change, even when the individual is highly motivated to change; old ideas, feelings and ways persist, and some sense of loss occurs in relinquishing them for the new; (2) Since change always produces some stress, current disorder, uncertainties about the future, and fantasies about losses incurred, it is necessary for individuals to have meaningful interpersonal nurture and emotional support during the process of changing, and until equilibrium is again established, if change is to be successfully achieved and maintained; (3) Facts, rationality, reasoned arguments alone are insufficient to effect change in individuals, for the emotional elements which resist the anxiety-producing disequilibrium will not yield to a rational approach alone; (4) There are usually some unanticipated consequences of change—consequences which affect not only the individual who is changing, but others related to him; (5) In many instances, individuals can change only through the help of a person or persons outside his own 'system'; (the teacher is a good example of such an agent of change); (6) If the individual, small group, organization and society are to survive in a world whose only constant is change, then consistent and serious attention must be devoted to ways of maintaining flexibility within the necessary stability of each of these systems, and of identifying with the adaptive process which can take constant change into account and meet it.

Within this larger context of the meaning of change to human beings, we think then of the process of education as one important type of change process. All of the major themes listed above would apply to education. Certainly it is true that as we learn, even though we are highly motivated towards learning, giving up old ideas, feelings, patterns of behaviour connotes some loss to us, especially when the new is not yet well established. We are all familiar with the heightened anxiety in ourselves and others as we try to take on the new in learning, as we try to change our old ways; we are familiar, too, with the need for strong identification with one or more persons who have what we are attempting to learn, the need for peers to help us cope with the new, to re-assure us in certain ways, to support us as we change. And even though, in the learning-teaching situation, rationality is essential and valuable, we know we do not learn by facts alone, but feelings about the facts and their effects on us pervade the learning.

[1] Bennis, Benne, and Chin, *op. cit.*, pp. 560–3.

I suppose that we have never yet been able to predict or to anticipate all the consequences of a particular learning experience for ourselves and others, and with all of the preceding stresses and consequences in mind, it is no wonder that we hear ourselves and others say, time after time, that we never would have learned this or that without the help of a teacher who 'saw us through'—who, in a sense, supported the positive side of the ambivalence (while recognizing the negative), and expected results—and somehow, we changed and met the expectations. In this as learners, we identify and utilize the adaptive powers within ourselves, within the small group, the organization, or society, and thus within the context of stability, maintain the flexibility to learn—to change.

What then, of Tyler's definition? In essence, it expresses a kind of combination of these themes of change. Education is a process of changing the behaviour patterns of people. Behaviour patterns include thinking, feeling and overt action—the acting, thinking, feeling human being. There is a rather wonderful aphorism which states in a pithy question the essential quality of the unifying implications of Tyler's definition—how do I know what I think until I feel what I do? In the educative process there can be no dichotomy between the conceptual and the feeling aspects of learning and of teaching. This is perhaps especially true when we recognize that we are dealing with learners who must learn to act helpfully (with competent knowledge and with appropriate feeling) in working with people who are experiencing problems in their social functioning. Can the small educational group, in its own way, reflect the thinking, feeling and doing of the learners who comprise it? I think the small educational group can be a laboratory for facilitating change in individual learners, and can also be a laboratory for the learners to try out the changes which each is striving to effect and to make his own.

If we agree with Tyler's definition that educational objectives should be expressed in terms which identify the kind of behaviour to be developed in the learner and the content or area of life in which this behaviour is to operate,[1] we can see again that the educational group can support or hinder the achievement of such objectives, and that the teacher must give attention to the on-going relationships and develop skills of intervening purposefully and effectively in line with diagnostic assessment and educational goals. Small groups can initiate and support change in individuals and in their own group structure and functioning; they can also support and increase resistance to change in individuals,

[1] Tyler, *op. cit.*, pp. 30–3.

and can very effectively develop a kind of group-generated resistance which can quite ruthlessly destroy the effectiveness of the finest educational objectives. The teacher must be able to diagnose and to deal with both motivation towards change and accompanying resistance to change inherent in individuals who are learning, and to recognize and deal with the group-engendered forces towards or resistances against change in individuals and in the group structure and functioning. Some problem-generating forces of resistance are quite directly accessible to modification and control in the educational group if the teacher is sensitive to the nature of what is going on within the group as an entity, and is able to utilize clues of behavioural evidence in the group to diagnose at greater depth what is happening to the individual learner.

Thus far I have tried to identify what I consider to be essential and relevant theoretical groundings for those who wish to understand and utilize the small group more effectively in learning and teaching. There are major lifetime pursuits involved in continuously trying to keep abreast of these theoretical developments and formulations, to select the relevant from them, and then to engage in the still more demanding task required if we are to integrate and to apply the concepts, propositions and theories drawn from the behavioural sciences, even within the segment devoted to small group research and theory, and within the segment devoted to how learning (or behavioural change) occurs in individuals, and how small groups can facilitate or hinder these changes. In this paper, my brief reference to each of these bodies of behavioural science theory is for the purpose of acknowledging these as essential and central ingredients for long and continuing study by many of us who are theory-oriented social practitioners (social workers and teachers of social workers). I have merely touched a small surface of what must be learned and dealt with, but every person who wishes to use this growing knowledge as a teacher must learn the content and try to use it in his own teaching. It is my aim to suggest these two major segments of content—small group concepts and learning (change) theory, particularly referring to small groups, in facilitating and supporting change in individuals. I hope the taste of knowledge and some insight into the potentials of how this theory can help the teacher will whet your appetites for the rigorous individual study which this theoretical under-pinning demands.

Within the context, then, of the small group in learning and teaching, and of the recognized theoretical matrix previously designated, I now turn to explore the first of the two major questions posed for this paper: If we believe that the task of an educational group is individual learning, how can a small group, formed for educational purposes, facilitate and enhance the learning of the individuals who comprise it? How can the small group help to effect and to support behavioural changes (which include changes in thinking, feeling, and doing) in line with educational objectives?

It is impossible to talk about the learning group until we say something quite crucial about the teacher. Such a question as we have just posed, pre-supposes a very important quality of relationship between the teacher and the group of learners. A small group can facilitate and enhance the learning of the individuals only if the teacher believes that members can learn from each other as well as from him, and only if the teacher, in a vital sense, trusts the group and thus entrusts to the members certain functions of learning from and teaching each other. In many ways this sounds quite obvious, and perhaps it seems even absurd to mention it. But it is not easy to learn to trust the group, and the exact meaning and consequences of this idea are not always clear.

If the teacher trusts the group, it does not mean that the teacher abandons the authority of position, knowledge and responsibility which is his to carry and to work out in the educational service of the learners. In fact, a teacher who abandons this authority or pretends it is not there only adds to the learning anxiety and increases the hostility and ambivalence of the learners. In addition, they mistrust a teacher who abandons or pretends to discard his rightful and responsible use of authority of knowledge and experience. There is a relationship of course between trust of the group and trust of the teacher. Basically, the teacher must trust the group members to be (or at least to become) able to help each other to learn, to teach each other, to learn from each other—in other words, to carry their responsible role as a learning group in the collaborative process of learning and teaching. Thus the teacher who trusts the learning group retains his responsibility for direction of educational content and process, and in addition, assumes responsibility for additional knowledge, taking into account and utilizing the inter-action process. When the teacher attempts to establish and maintain relationships which reduce anxieties, defensiveness and resistances in the learners, the learners can be more open to learning, and more learning and change will take place. If the learners come to feel that the teacher will help them with revealed inadequacies and will not destroy them because of revealed inadequacies, they will become more willing to bring inadequacies into view.

The teacher who trusts the learning group learns from them—different knowledge and understanding from that which he is teaching them, but often a kind of insight and self-knowledge which is an invaluable part of a teacher's professional self. How then, can the small group facilitate individual learning, help to effect and to support behavioural changes in line with our educational objectives? I should like to suggest and to develop briefly some seven major ways. These are drawn from our current 'knowns' about small groups, confirmed both experientially and by research, and applied to the small group which has educational goals and tasks to perform.[1]

(1) A small group in which he becomes comfortable and to which he feels he belongs can help an individual learner open himself to learning. Under these given conditions he can find it possible to bring to the surface his needs for knowledge and his problems in learning. Thoughts, feelings, behaviour must be surfaced in order to be amenable to change. In such a small group, it may become possible for the individual learner to listen to and to accept relevant reactions from other learners (as well as from the teacher) about his ideas, feelings and behaviour. It becomes possible for individuals to encourage others to participate, and some individuals who are unable to respond to the teacher's encouragement can respond to the encouragement from their peers.

We know that learning, particularly of an attitudinal or emotional nature, is facilitated by this type of group membership—in fact, we think that such membership is more of a necessity than a convenience if attitude change is to occur. Individuals learn not only by doing, but by seeking reactions to revealed ideas, feelings and behaviour. The individual must feel that he is being heard clearly and completely, for development and not for destruction.

(2) A small group can help the individual learner to gain methods of experimenting, analysing and utilizing experiences and knowledge resulting from his problem solving efforts. The group can be a kind of laboratory to try out new ways of thinking, feeling and acting.

(3) A small group can help to supply understanding, support and

---

[1] In this section of the paper I am heavily indebted to three articles appearing in *The Planning of Change* edited by Warren Bennis, Kenneth Benne, and Robert Chin, previously cited. The article by Leland P. Bradford, 'The Teaching-Learning Transaction', pp. 493–502, Kurt Lewin's and Paul Grabbe's article on 'Principles of Re-Education', pp. 503–509, and Dorwin Cartwright's and Ronald Lippitt's article on 'Group Dynamics and the Individual', pp. 264–77, have contributed in a major way to the development of this section. I should also like to cite a small gem of a book—Jerome S. Bruner, *The Process of Education*, Harvard University Press, Cambridge, Massachusetts, 1962, which stretched my own thinking about education to a degree for which I am immensely grateful.

correctives (in knowledge, feelings and actions) and thus the inter-dependence aspects are maximized and used, and not the dependence on authority aspects alone. In this way, each learner contributes to as well as takes from the group. He can increase his own understanding of how others perceive his ideas, feelings and behaviour—a most crucial kind of understanding for an individual to acquire.

(4) If the small group is cohesive, it provides effective support for the learner in his encounters with anxiety-provoking aspects of learning. This is not to say that the group removes or erases individual anxiety (nor do we want that to happen, for no learning would take place without individual anxiety), but the group does tend to help the individual to cope with anxiety and to render it manageable and educationally useful. The group membership itself can offer direct satisfaction, and this satisfaction in membership has a generalized effect of anxiety—reduction to more manageable proportions.

(5) A small group which is strong does not need to suppress differences. It is the insecure, threatened group which cannot tolerate and fears difference. While all groups tend to promote conformity, they do not all tend to promote uniformity—they can, for instance, promote conformity to hetero-geneity—to the value of individual difference as well as to the value of commonalities. There is a quality of inter-dependence between well integrated individuals and cohesive groups which value and support differences as well as likenesses.

(6) A small group can be an anchorage for planning how to utilize in the actual work situation the learning which was achieved in the educational group. In a sense, this is an educational problem of forming a bridge between the learning group (a kind of island where certain changes occurred) and the mainland of the work situation—a problem of transfer of learning and maintenance of change or gains made. The act of talking through such changes and problems of maintenance can aid the later maintenance of change. This application of change in the learner's usual situation is often a far more difficult task than the initial learning and change which take place in a more protected situation. It is to be expected that some regression and loss will occur. Group attention to this problem can help.

(7) A small group can be a resource for developing a continuing system of learning on the part of each individual learner. This, too, means the use of the learning group for individual planning. The group can sometimes allow the individual to go further more easily by him-self when he returns to his own work situation, again maintaining and

even facilitating further change and his own future problem-solving ability.

We turn now to the second major aspect for exploration—the small group in teaching. In one sense, I suppose, this could be thought of as simply 'the other side of the coin' and all we have emphasized before could be appropriately stated in the form of requirements for the teacher if he is to take the group into account when he teaches.

However, I would like to push beyond this, and make an effort to suggest some principles which are in a sense principles of practice for the teacher in working with a small group of learners. These principles might well be thought of as directed towards supplying at least some answers to the question: how can the teacher make conscious use of the small group structure and dynamics to develop individual and group educational diagnoses, and to facilitate and enhance the teaching process (emphasizing that the learning-teaching process is inter-actional or transactional in essence)?

We must recognize first of all, that the teacher must be clear on educational objectives and on the content to be taught in order to be free to see and hear the reactions and inter-actions of the learners, to 'read' them accurately (to use our current space jargon) and to assess their meaning for individual learning. The teacher must be able to connect himself in a meaningful way, both at the thinking level and at the interactional (or intervention) level, with each learner as an individual, with the several as a group or entity, and with the structure and dynamics of the interactions among the learners and with him. At the same time he must retain his responsible part for direction of the teaching content, of the group process, and of his own professional use of himself towards the meeting of the educational objectives. If the teacher is unfamiliar with or uncomfortable with the teaching content, and must therefore invest a great deal of emotional energy in trying to master it or in concern lest he be 'caught short' in this aspect, he cannot be free to let his thoughts and feelings really take the learners into account. He may miss, then, the verbal and non-verbal communications of the learners, and may miss what their reactions and inter-actions can tell him. He may miss the meaning of silence of an individual or of the group, or he may miss the source of the resistance which seems suddenly to have appeared. For educational diagnosis that is meaningful, intelligent, and useful, all these must be taken into account.

If the teacher has an opportunity to decide upon or to make

suggestions about the composition of the learning group, he is faced with a technical problem of some difficulty. Small group research and theory, and practice experience offer as yet no final answers, but strong support from these sources can be found for composing our small learning groups in the way most 'real life' groups form—with some likeness and some difference, a blend of similarities and variations, of homogeneity and heterogeneity. This, of course, does not tell us a great deal, except that there must indeed be some bond which the members themselves deem important—and that along with the commonality must go some 'spice of difference for alternatives' which can act as a stimulant at some times and a leavening agent at others. A balance of likeness and of difference seems to provide some built-in disequilibrium in the group—an essential for change. It also provides by very composition the growth or learning experience which can occur through an individual's learning not only to support but to value difference, at the same time that some support and identification with likeness becomes possible. Thus it does not become necessary for the individual learners and the teacher to homogenize the group nor to make a fetish of difference.

As we have previously pointed out, it is essential for the teacher to formulate a diagnostic assessment at two levels—an educational diagnosis of each individual learner and a group diagnosis which indicates how each individual is or is not utilizing the group in learning, and how the group is or is not facilitating the learning of the individual members. As he assesses the structure and functioning of the group he uses the concepts of group structure, goals, interpersonal relations, group controls, group cohesion and morale, and group norms as the lenses through which he can examine the group more closely. It is essential in an education group that the group processes and development contribute to rather than detract from the learning progress of individuals.

As the teacher attempts to assess the group structure and functioning, it may help him to know that he can expect certain processes to go on, sometimes in ways more subtle or hidden but at other times in ways quite obvious and sometimes disturbing or distracting. I would suggest some half dozen of these processes or phases which seem to occur quite regularly. Each of these exemplifies the fact that a group works on tasks and relationships at the same time.

(1) First of all, in every group of learners the teacher can expect an initial period when the learners will actively (or perhaps in some instances more passively) feel out and test the teacher and each other,

trying to find some basis for determining how comfortable or un-comfortable this particular learning situation is going to be, trying to find some 'predictables' in the unknown, trying to 'structure' it to make it less strange and less threatening. A good bit of emotional energy goes into this testing, even in its less obvious forms, and we have a good example of a group working on the task (learning content) and concomitantly on the relationships which have a great deal to do with how the learner will be able to learn. The group will inevitably go through periods of some greater or less disorganization. This is essential to change—and often, as with an individual, a crisis is productive of learning.

(2) We have previously mentioned the ambivalence involved in learning, and in a small group, a teacher can usually expect some resistance to the learning-teaching 'contract' or agreement, no matter how it is defined. To become a member of a learning group, an individual must give up some of exactly what he wants at the time he wants it in order to derive the benefits which accrue from the contri-butions of others. Such accommodation does not always come readily, and individuals may express their discomfort or ambivalence in varied forms. One of the facts of small group life is that no one individual can ever have all he wants of the other members or of the teacher, and this fact cannot be circumvented.

(3) The teacher can expect some struggle for place among the learners, some competition for a special relationship with him, some-times some attempts by individuals or sub-groups to wall him off or isolate him from the rest and 'keep' him for themselves. He can expect to see among the learners the rise of central figures whose influence towards or away from the accomplishment of educational objectives is most crucial.

(4) The group processes can aid in working out the ambivalence and resistance. If the teacher is able to tolerate the expression of negative as well as positive feelings, the ambivalence and resistance can be worked through much more readily. If the teacher or most of the group members have too much anxiety concerning hostility to authority, the group may focus on a weak or deviant person in the group and make of him a scapegoat. It is possible for the teacher to handle such scapegoating by helping the learners to express their hostility more directly instead of displacing it, and by holding to the educational goals, engaging the group in conscious awareness of these goals and of the group as a means to facilitate individual learning. The learners often develop a common bond of affection for each other and for the

teacher, but it is quite usual in educational groups that some ambivalence can be expected to persist throughout. The demands of learning can never quite be met, and while the learners want to meet them, the changes required are likely to be tinged with some continuing ambivalent feelings.

(5) The teacher must sharpen his sensitivity to how the learners perceive his behaviour and to the consequences of his behaviour in the group of learners. We know that learners are extremely sensitive to consistency in the teacher, who must be able to convey and to demonstrate again and again—as the teacher, I am here for each of you and for all of you at one and the same time. Along with this, learners are ultra-sensitive to fairness in the teacher—to the recognition of what is fair to each within the context of what is fair to all. We sometimes think of this as more important with children, but this concept and the standard or norm implied have meaning to all learners.

(6) If the educational goal is for individual learners to grow in ability to solve problems and to carry that improved ability beyond the learning group and into their own work situations, then the teacher must work in ways consistent with this goal—in ways which demonstrate respect and concern for each individual as a learner and for the interactional and transactional aspects of the learning-teaching situation and educative process, as well as respect and concern for the content to be learned and taught. Some recent research into small group learning-teaching situations has produced two major findings which are of special concern to those of us who teach social workers. When the teacher was free to take into account and to utilize effectively the group interaction towards facilitating educational objectives (1) there was substantial evidence that the learners could focus on the problems being discussed; there was evidence of decreased interpersonal anxiety; there was evidence of greater integration of content by the learners, and ability to state and elaborate principles in a context meaningful for their work; (2) there was marked evidence of communication of feeling as well as exchange of information and knowledge; there was evidence that the learners had increased their clinical insight into the dynamics of the case under consideration; there was substantial evidence of freedom to focus diagnostic thinking and to give creative consideration to possible treatment plans which might be utilized by the learners themselves in helping the person in difficulty.[1]

[1] A. Paul Hare, *Handbook of Small Group Research*, The Free Press, Glencoe, Illinois, 1962, p. 333.

The meaning of such findings for our ways of work in teaching small groups of social workers seems so clear as to need no further comment.

There now remains the task of bringing together that which we have temporarily separated for purposes of exploration and analysis. Our concern is with learning and teaching as interactive processes, and with the small group as the central term. The group of learners and the teacher come together by educational 'contract' which consists in essence of and is bounded by the educational objectives. In order to achieve the educational objectives, the individual goals of the learners, the group goal (helping the individuals to learn, and in a sense, the teacher to teach) and the teaching goals of the teacher must find some common, agreed upon ground within the educational objectives and the goals must be re-worked by learners and teacher together in the on-going interaction of the educative process. The goals of each learner, of the group, of the teacher must be clear, well defined, and in line with educational objectives—or else much emotional energy and a great deal of anxiety on the part of learners and of the teacher will go into the search for goals and for meaningful congruence and common ground, rather than into ways of work together to achieve clearly defined, agreed upon, workable goals, known to each and to all.

And now a word about the teacher and the small group of learners. All of us have known excellent teachers who intuitively seem to know and to be able to practice that kind of teaching-learning involvement and skill with their students which (to paraphrase Bruner slightly)[1] brings about the 'sense of freedom to explore possibilities, the devotion to elegant solutions, and the interplay among the learners that, in effect, make each learner stronger as a learner' than he would be individually. The intuitive and the artistic must ever be within the person of the teacher in the act of teaching. But for most of us, the freeing of the use of intuition to go beyond the commonplace as a teacher rests upon a solid foundation of knowledge. It is with this belief and commitment that I have suggested some outlines of current knowledge of the small group in facilitating change in individuals, some outlines which I hope will intrigue you towards discovery of deeper substance which can develop and become real only on the basis of your own pursuit, involvement, and effort. In short, the full potential of the small group in learning and teaching remains for each of you to discover and to make your own.

[1] Jerome S. Bruner, *op. cit.*, p. 11.

Suggested Reading: The Small Group in Learning and Teaching

1. Eileen A. Blackey, *Group Leadership in Staff Training.* U.S. Department of Health, Education, and Welfare, Washington, D.C. 1957.
2. Leland P. Bradford, 'The Teaching-Learning Transaction' in *The Planning of Change* (Warren G. Bennis, Kenneth D. Benne, Robert Chin, eds.). Holt, Rinehart and Winston, New York, 1962, pp. 493–502; or in *Adult Education,* Vol. VIII, No. 3, Spring, 1948, pp. 135–45, published by the Adult Education Association of the U.S.A., 743 North Wabash Avenue, Chicago 11, Illinois.
3. Dorwin Cartwright and Alvin Zander. 'Introduction to Group Dynamics—Origins, Issues and Basic Assumptions', in *Group Dynamics—Research and Theory* (Dorwin Cartwright and Alvin Zander, eds.), Row, Petersen and Company, Evanston, Illinois (Second Edition), 1960, pp. 3–65.
4. Dorwin Cartwright, 'Achieving Change in People' in *The Planning of Change* (Warren G. Bennis, Kenneth D. Benne, Robert Chin, eds.). Holt, Rinehart and Winston, New York, 1962, pp. 698–706 or in *Human Relations,* Vol. XIV, No. 4, 1951, pp. 381–92.
5. Grace Longwell Coyle, 'The Role of the Teacher in the Creation of An Integrated Curriculum', *Social Work Journal,* Vol. XXXIII, No. 2, April, 1952 and 'New Insights Available to the Social Worker from the Social Sciences', *ibid.,* Vol. XXXIII, No. 3, September, 1952; *Social Process in the Community and Group,* Council on Social Work Education, New York, 1958 and *Social Science in the Professional Education of Social Workers,* Council on Social Work Education, New York, 1958.
6. Kurt Lewin and Paul Grabbe, 'Principles of Re-Education' in *The Planning of Change* (Warren G. Bennis, Kenneth D. Benne, Robert Chin, eds). Holt, Rinehart and Winston, New York, 1962, pp. 503–509, or as 'Conduct, Knowledge and Acceptance of New Values' in his *Resolving Social Conflicts,* Harper and Bros., New York, 1948.
7. George E. Miller, M.D., 'The Teacher Teaches' and 'Basic Techniques of Instruction—the Lecture and Group Discussion' in *Teaching and Learning in Medical School.* (George E. Miller, M.D., ed.), Harvard University Press, Cambridge, Massachusetts, 1961, pp. 65–72 and 95–116.
8. Michael S. Olmsted, *The Small Group.* Random House, New York, 1959.

9. Helen Harris Perlman, 'Teaching Casework by the Discussion Method', *Social Service Review*, XXIV, September, 1950, 334–46, and 'The Lecture as a Method in Teaching Casework', *ibid.*, XXV, March, 1951, pp. 19–32. Both reproduced in this present volume, pp. 98 and 110 respectively.

10. W. J. H. Sprott, *Human Groups*. Pelican Books, A–346, 1958.

11. Charlotte Towle, 'Basic Learning Principles', 'Personality Development', 'Personality Development and the Integration of Learning', 'Educational Principles and Process', in *The Learner in Education for the Professions*. The University of Chicago Press, Chicago, Illinois, 1954, pp. 23–174.

12. Ralph W. Tyler, 'Implications of Research in the Behavioural Sciences for Group Life and Group Services', *The Social Welfare Forum*, 1960. Columbia University Press, New York, 1960, pp. 113–26.

3

THE TEACHER IN EDUCATION FOR SOCIAL WORK*

EILEEN YOUNGHUSBAND

IT is significant that the various professions which have developed during this century have all passed or are passing through certain characteristic processes as each one struggles to emerge from set rules or large aspirations to the stage of professional judgment, with application of principles and general theories to specific practice. It is commonly agreed that a profession must have not only a substantial basis of knowledge which is verifiable, has high predictive value, and is applicable in a range of circumstances but also that its practitioners must be able to combine and apply this knowledge to problems within the field of the particular profession. They must indeed be able to use their knowledge and skill with human feeling, coupled with artistry and judgment in each unique situation. Moreover, in a time of great social change and breathless scientific advance, professional education must equip students with sufficient certainty for today's practice but with the capacity to live with uncertainty without losing their sense of direction, and with zest for unlearning as well as for new learning.

The professions face three questions: Why train? For what? and How do adult students learn? Any design for professional education which neglects to struggle with these three questions in combination will fail in its task. As far as social work education in the United Kingdom is concerned, we have invested most of our thought in the question of what to teach. This is good in itself compared with the vagueness of two or three decades ago, when we relied on wide generalizations from an alarming sweep of the social sciences taught without much application to real life problems, coupled—or not coupled—with all too specific practice. The result was that any relation between theory and practice was almost purely coincidental. Nowadays there is a better understanding that those who teach in any professional course must struggle to select from that profession's

* Inaugural Eileen Younghusband Lecture, given at the National Institute for Social Work Training, London, June, 1967. Published in *The Social Service Review*, Vol. 41, No. 4, December, 1967.

supporting sciences those aspects closest to its application and must combine the most relevant material from several sciences to focus these more sharply on the problems with which the profession deals. It is all too easy to stop at this point, but it is nonetheless vital to take the next step—to distil from these sciences and from systematic study of professional practice a methodology which can be transmitted to students, both in the classroom and in field practice. This practice theory should, of course, have predictive value. But in social work the fun begins when we try to bring these broad principles down to earth.

We still seem satisfied to imagine that answers to questions about the purpose of training and how people learn will somehow emerge from deciding what the content of education should be. The result is that not enough effort is put into trying to discover what a newly qualified social worker must know and be able to do; yet unless we know what we are aiming to produce at the end, how can we really know what the content and priorities of the course should be and what educational methods will enable students to learn with the maximum use of their capacities and the minimum of wasted effort?

Failure to grapple with the hard task of defining and constantly evaluating objectives can result in our not having yardsticks by which to measure the success of students, other than their ability to absorb and reproduce what they have learned in the course. So the process comes full cycle. But in this event we have few means of knowing what parts of the students' learning were relevant, partially relevant, or perhaps irrelevant to their subsequent development as professional people; what they will retain because they can go on using it and what they will forget because it is not usable by them. Along with the assumption that we can decide *a priori* what ought to be the content of education for social work goes a strange lack of curiosity about what constitutes good practice in social work itself and what social demands it should be equipped to meet, tomorrow as well as today. We have some pious generalizations, some analyses of how social workers actually spend their time, a very few studies by individual social workers of their complex tasks, and the studies of probation by the Home Office Research Unit. But we do not know in precise and comprehensive terms what are, or should be, the elements in the best social work practice, or what administrative structures and organizational arrangements would enable this practice to be most successfully deployed in the service of the people who need it.

'In my end is my beginning' should be the motto of all who teach social work students. It is only the end that can cast light on the means, that should determine the content of education for social work, the weight that should be given to different aspects of the course, how much of what should be taught when, by what method, and for what purpose. (Incidentally, this is also a reason why social work teachers should have the final say in what is taught by specialists). None of this is static. It should be subjected to constant, built-in evaluation of the effectiveness of every element in the course in its relation to all the others.

I do not want for a moment to suggest that the whole of a profession is comprised in good practice, far less in teaching 'know-how'. There are social work functions which are no part of method as such. We must also equip students with a way of working and a natural habit of asking apposite questions which ensures that they will go on learning. There should be in any profession a commitment to research, a concern with social policy and with relevant social action. Moreover, values and a philosophy are as much part of any profession's way of life as respect for knowledge. Different students have very different temperaments, and not all will come out at the end full-fledged professional paragons. But it is the responsibility of social work teachers, as of professional associations, to help them all to be conscious that the nature of their professional commitment does not stop with the caseworker's use of relationship.

Obviously, in any professional education it is not possible to do more than give students enough to be getting on with; to start with sufficient momentum so that they are likely to continue on the right lines. The right line is, of course, not a party line, but a basis of knowledge and competence, together with a sense of direction and purpose, a conception of the nature of social work which also leaves the student clear about the importance of values and of keeping abreast of social change and disruptive new learning, as well as concentrating on becoming more skilled in day-to-day practice. As Charlotte Towle once put it in a talk to graduating students: 'It is only as you master something rather than merely entertain many things that you will have made what you have learned your own. What is your own you can use freely—to depart from the established order.'[1]

Here is a massive educational task, made all the greater by the constant dilemma that faces us at the present time of quantity versus quality. This dilemma is falsely stated if by it we mean either training

---

[1] Charlotte Towle, Talk given at a Convocation Luncheon, at the School of Social Service Administration, Chicago, 1957 (unpublished).

D

a large number of students at a low level or a small number at a higher level. We are probably giving too many people too short a training and certainly investing too little of our resources in discovering how to train at a more advanced level of both theory and practice. But that is another story. The point at the moment is that no matter what the level, the training should be, educationally speaking, the best possible for the purpose. There is no reason why a course in a college of further education should not be just as good, though not just the same, as a university course, as far as educational planning and teaching are concerned. But we must be clear about a manageable range of objectives and the means necessary for their attainment.

'How?' as well as 'What?' are of equal importance. Our failure to analyse what good practice means has been matched by lack of sufficient interest in how adult students learn, compared with concentration on what we think they should be taught. What they are taught is sometimes an uneasy compromise between social work teachers and some lecturers in other subjects who are more interested in teaching a basic course than in discovering what social work students need and how to relate different subjects effectively to each other. For instance, a course in law may be almost purely factual and a concurrent course in sociology contain nothing about law as a form of social control and an expression of social attitudes. The result is that sometimes so-called integrating seminars have to help students to see the interrelations between one subject and another when initial joint planning in the light of objectives could have prevented these watertight compartments from the beginning. Also, the length of a course is often determined by expediency, while the range, depth, balance and interrelation of its content, of the different parts of the course, may bear no examined relation to the students' capacities for understanding, absorption and retention.

What is crucial is not what students are taught but what they learn. The way adults learn obviously differs in some ways from the way children learn. For instance, the wider experience of adults is a very cause of their greater inflexibility, since previous responses have laid down attitudes and habits, largely unconscious or taken for granted, which result in resistance to change. But conversely, adults are clearer than children about their long-term as well as their short-term goals. We need much more knowledge about the light which this fact and other elements in the psychology of learning cast on educational experiences that produce the most creative learning in adults.

The implications of these questions suggest many problems to which we do not know the answers. Nonetheless, we know enough from our collective experience in social work practice and teaching to ask significant questions and to keep records of our observations. Records are already being kept piecemeal by some individual social work teachers. But what we need is a systematic plan for observation, for the formulation of hypotheses, and for their testing by alternative methods in various educational situations. This could be a fruitful co-operative enterprise, sponsored by the various training councils, the National Institute for Social Work Training, and the professional associations.

To turn now to another aspect of learning, most social work students have a strong desire to learn in that they want to become social workers and to master whatever knowledge and competence is relevant to their aim. This desire sounds splendid, but it poses difficult educational problems. Students are highly motivated to learn what they regard as relevant, but they do not necessarily know what *is* relevant or see the relevance of all that they are taught. Alternatively, they accept uncritically what their teachers provide. In neither instance do they really make it part of themselves.

Faculty members responsible for designing and teaching courses face a series of challenges. It is essential to reinforce and channel motivation, but this means helping students to see why they are studying particular parts of certain subjects and how different aspects of the course fit together and reinforce each other; what they are expected to do with each part of it; and how they can achieve whatever is the appropriate mastery. Students must have opportunities to question and criticize, in short, to toss everything around until they have either made it their own or rejected it. Faculty members must know how to free students to learn, to help them overcome whatever may be their individual blocks to learning. With some students such release results in a dramatic leap forward in perception and ability to learn. The teacher is forced to think out what he teaches, why he thinks it important for the students, and what he expects them to do with it. And thus, incidentally, to reflect on how much of the subject is essential for any given purpose. If this is not done and the results constantly discussed with them, students may sometimes be quite right to discard irrelevant or badly timed material that leaves them confused and frustrated. Some academics are infuriated by the often too glib saying that in professional education knowledge is for use. As A. N. Whitehead put it: 'Pedants sneer at an education which is useful. But if education is not useful, what is it? Is it a talent to be hidden away in a napkin?'

The discipline of priorities, of subordinating one's absorption in the subject to students' needs, is hard for those teachers whose interest in their subject exceeds their interest in how students learn and for what purposes. We need to be aware of the multiple meanings of the word 'use'. A scholar is no doubt concerned with knowledge useful to him in enlarging his subject. But a professional person's primary interest is in knowledge and modes of application that will help him to deal more effectively with problems in his particular field of practice. All teachers in social work education, as in other professions, have an obligation to help students perceive more accurately the nature of the task and assimilate the range of knowledge that casts the most searching light upon its components. To do so is not easy for curriculum planners when each of the social and behavioural sciences is a substantial field of study in its own right and when common frames of reference between them are lacking. One of the many unsolved problems in social work curriculum construction is how to do justice to the integrity of each subject and yet select from and interrelate the most relevant parts in order to give social work students a more profound, accurate and usable understanding of man as he lives and interacts with his human and physical environment. Nonetheless, there are some unifying themes that help to provide coherence and unity. These are now commonly taught in the best-planned courses. They are themes like the basic human drives and their social manifestations, the range and consequences of social deviance, the importance of the early years of life, problems of priorities in social provision, reconciling the good of the individual with the good of society, the effect of economic factors on people's ways of life, the changing values of an 'open' society, and a number of others. There are also unifying principles related to values, on the one hand, and to methods of study, on the other.

A clue to selection of the most relevant subject matter lies in an actual rather than an aspirational assessment of good social work practice, with particular attention to fruitful growing points. A simple illustration will make this clear. In one course students were said to have spent some time studying the structure and functions of the middle ear, indeed to have been examined in their knowledge of it, although it is to be hoped in their later careers as social workers they never did anything so dangerous as to use this knowledge. Probably

<hr/>

[1] A. N. Whitehead, *The Aims of Education and Other Essays*, Ernest Benn, London, 1962, p. 3.

the only useful thing they could do with it was to forget its details and retain what one demonstration might have taught them.

Knowledge which gives better understanding is obviously knowledge for use, for instance, the concept of role or grasping why children need to play. On another dimension, clarity about the difference between a scientific concept and a value judgment is knowledge for use. But knowledge which results in intellectual understanding is, as we all know, not the same thing as ability to apply it, particularly in the untidy drama of human life.

In attempts to look first at what is the aim of the course, and in the light of this to struggle to clarify what students must know and be competent to do, we soon face dilemmas of part-whole learning, of watertight compartments, and of how to keep knowledge and its application closely related to each other—in short, the perennial problems not only of selection but also of what is best taught when and by what means. In the United Kingdom we have a number of interesting variations in total course design but no comparative studies to try to determine which produces the best results, according to some objective criteria of effectiveness. We have, for example, courses on the following patterns: three years of study for a degree in social studies, followed by one year of related theory and practice; four-year integrated degree courses; three years for a degree in another subject, followed by one and one-half or two years of related theory and practice; or two years of combined theory and practice without a preliminary degree in related or unrelated subjects. On the face of it, students with a social studies degree followed by or integrated with a university professional education ought to do better than others in the long if not in the short run. But do they? Conversely, the two-year students should be the least well-equipped for the professional task. But are they? What has each got that the other lacks? And how could the best in the educational experience of each be appropriately transferred to the other and the most wasteful eliminated? In one pattern a solid base of social studies, with some training in scientific method, is laid before professional studies begin. In another, students have a university education, but social studies and professional material are interwoven, with the result that theoretical knowledge is quickly applied. In the third there may be almost no base of adult education on which to build.

What effects do these variations have? What is the difference or the close relationship between being a well-educated person and a good professional worker? To what extent are the two interwoven?

What price are we paying for each? What pattern would give us the best possible returns, educationally and professionally? What does it take for someone to become an educated person, blessed with wisdom, culture and understanding of the world in which he lives? Can we produce such people by taking thought, or must we ultimately depend on the good or bad fairies at the baby's cradle? We are probably spending over £1,000,000 a year on the education of social workers, yet we have little more than inspired guesses or strongly held views about the answers to such questions as these and many others.

These different patterns of education and training contain examples of part-whole learning. Do students learn most effectively by first studying one or more of the social sciences as separate disciplines, with any one of these first explored in its own right so that they have a clear grasp of its essence and structure and are able to describe, analyse, and classify the phenomena with which it deals? If they have so studied, will they be more able to relate several social and behavioural sciences and focus them on particular problems? Or are these processes, taught in isolated succession, too remote from each other so that there is comparatively little carry-over from one to the other? Conversely, teaching which starts by focusing different disciplines upon a series of social problems like illegitimacy, delinquency, poverty, housing, social security and the like, and then works outwards, may leave the students with insufficient grasp of the essential nature of each discipline and without conceptual tools for further learning.

If the answer is neither part nor whole learning as such, but learning wholes by constant application and illustration, then what light is cast both on our present arrangements and on the best design for any particular professional course? 'Best,' of course, includes economy of effort, time and resources in relation to the desired end results. Whitehead wrote that 'the really useful training yields a comprehension of a few general principles with a thorough grounding in the way they apply to a variety of concrete details.'[1] But in social work education we have not yet achieved systematic identification of these general principles or discovered what and how thorough grounding students need in their application. For example, it is relatively easy to grasp the principles of economy of hypothesis and sufficient causation but students' field work placements do not always show shining examples of their application.

If the purpose of any given professional education is to bring about changes in the behaviour of the learner, then we must be clear about

[1] *op. cit.*, p. 42.

the desired behaviour changes, discover how they can be brought about, and decide how much change, over what range and depth is necessary. Whitehead's 'thorough grounding' is essential if learning and capacity to welcome new knowledge are to continue in the pressure of subsequent work situations, which may sometimes blight rather than nurture students' tender skill. As Ralph Tyler has said, we must give students sufficient practice of the desired behaviour. For instance, intellectual learning requires practice in all the necessary processes of description, classification, analysis, conceptualization and application. But these intellectual processes are more quickly mastered than a form of use which entails imaginative consideration in the appropriate application of knowledge to particular examples, coupled with the development of a matching range of skills. These two further processes are more complex, hence slower, and require more practice to produce the desired behaviour than intellectual learning on its own. Moreover, in a field like social work, the emotions are heavily engaged, and students also have to face their prejudiced personal value judgments and subject them to professional discipline. The singlemindedness of intellectual discovery is insufficient. But to be stretched intellectually and emotionally at the same time is very demanding, partly because the two learning rhythms are different, even though in the long run changes in thinking lead to changes in feeling and both are reinforced by application.

To understand this better it is necessary for us to look at the processes in learning any skill, with their implications for social work education. There are two elements in such learning: first, application of knowledge, or perception, followed by development of practice skills, or action. In social work education the appropriate use of knowledge in specific situations is partly learned through classroom discussion, but mainly through field work in social agencies. It is doubtful whether either of these methods as at present used permits students enough practice, coupled with quick feedback, to develop sufficient accuracy and sensitivity in the differential use and combination of knowledge, especially in the human sciences.

We have not taken into sufficient account that the first step in any skill learning is a reasonably accurate perception by the learner of the skill to be mastered. In many forms of skill learning this is achieved by demonstration by the teacher, in activities as different as learning to drive a car, toss a pancake, play the piano, or perform a surgical operation. Until the teacher and the learner have a common perception of the skill to be mastered, there are bound to be cross purposes that result in lack of progress. In social work, confusion is often apparent in supervisors' reports on students' first field placements. Yet social work teachers have given comparatively little attention to how to demonstrate clearly this crucial first step in skill learning. In a sense this is understandable, because social work is a complex series of connected activities, based largely on the use of relationships and thus dealing with intangibles. But this very fact makes it all the more necessary to help students to comprehend its nature fairly accurately as the first step before starting to practice. They can probably do this only by demonstration rather than through verbal exposition, which does not have sufficient significance or impact for them.

The next step in skill learning is for the learner to begin to practice at a level of complexity and span within his ability to grasp and to attempt to put into action. At this stage it is naturally important that good practice should be reinforced and bad practice quickly inhibited. Quick and accurate feedback is essential. At present it is provided by the often too slow and for this purpose rather cumbersome devices of process recording and supervisory discussion. I do not mean for one moment to suggest that these are not of great value for some purposes, but for certain aspects of skill learning, the time interval and the generality are both too large. It may be that some better devices will evolve from the use of tape recording and television of students' interviews, followed by quick playback and discussion. The day when this will be possible is not far off; indeed, it is already arriving in the United States. In the meantime new technical aids will emphasize but not meet the need for detailed analysis of field practice to discover how much and what kind of opportunities and what time intervals students need to begin to master desired skills. We need more certainty about the necessary range, level and content of direct relations with clients; other necessary abilities, like report-writing and interagency consultation; co-operation with members of other professions; ability to function in an administrative hierarchy, and so forth. We also need to know what length and type of practice in each of these in combination with the others is necessary to develop sufficient dependable competence in a newly qualified social worker. In particular, we do not know what amount of client contact, with what range of different people over the life history of different typical crises or forms of social work intervention is necessary to bring about a sufficient amalgam of theory and practice, a sufficient understanding of themselves and other people, in newly qualified social workers. Field teaching has improved immeasurably in the last twenty years, but overworked social work teachers and supervisors are still left to improve it further as best they may by their own efforts at a time of expansion, when every possible social agency and supervisor is having to be used. We spend large sums of public money in preparing social workers so that they may be competent to help people in acute distress or need, yet we spend practically nothing on trying to discover the most effective ways of learning, either in the classroom or in field practice.

There may be protests that to talk about the art of human relations in these terms is to reduce it to a series of techniques. That would be true if it were the whole story. It is part of the story, but in the analysis of a very complicated subject we must also study different individual learning patterns and the rhythm of learning, with its time intervals, its spurts, and its apparent regression followed by integration. There is also the dilemma of how to correlate carefully planned steps in skill learning with students' spontaneous, warmhearted desire to help, with individual insight and initiative, and with a wayward wisdom of the heart, which sometimes outstrips the plodding orderliness of the head.

Perhaps this is one reason why characteristic processes in learning a skill, the stages of perception followed by beginning practice with feedback and positive and negative reinforcement, usually lead sooner or later to the slough of despond, that difficult stage in which the learner's knowledge, his perception of good practice, and his desire for creative application far outstrip his abilities. He sees all too clearly when it is too late what was happening in an interview or group session, what he thinks he ought to have done or not done, or said or not said. And the clumsiness of what he actually did or failed to do mocks the imagined perfection of his performance. In social work the usual frustrations of this stage are added to by the growing awareness of self and others which is part of a more vivid understanding of human personality, desires and behaviour. At such times many students experience an almost unbearable disintegration, particularly if their cultural values and previous view of themselves and their family relationships also seem to be in the melting pot. Some will say that this is a necessary process, which shows that more elements in the personality are being brought within the central organizing system. To others it appears to be a consequence of poor educational method that has set up resistance through teaching which has resulted in mental indigestion and is rejected on intellectual or emotional grounds. In short, could learning in social work be so structured that a series of challenges always met with success, a success that gave the impetus to the next step? Or is the time lag between perception and performance, coupled with increased awareness of self and others, inevitably experienced at some stages as painful and frustrating?

All education is interwoven with subtle relationships between time and learning. For instance, we know that time intervals are needed after each learning episode if the content is to be absorbed. But this is a very general statement. We do not know what time intervals for what learning episodes or what type of learning or, for that matter, for what different student learning patterns. Certainly a period of mulling over seems to be a necessary element in all learning. It goes on inside the individual, but it must also be expressed, which is one of the many reasons why groups of students learn from each other. It is also a reason for class discussion which allows for verbal playing around with ideas, not least because, on the whole, students remember best what they themselves have said and thus made their own. Time and learning also have to do with the process of habit formation, which is an important element in all skill because it frees energy and attention for the development of more finely differentiated activity. The early stages of learning are slow just because little can be passed over to what William James called 'the effortless custody of habit' and because almost every step in a process must be consciously worked out and executed. Timing and speed of learning are also related to motivation, to the degree of the student's lively curiosity and educational sophistication, allied to the extent of his desire to learn, his zest in achievement, and whether his previous experience of himself as effective and competent is strengthened or questioned in a new situation. There is also the crucial question of how to keep the level of anxiety about right in teaching and learning, since too little or too much anxiety causes breakdown in learning. Indeed, two central tasks in education are to regulate anxiety and to develop realistic confidence. Zest for learning is perhaps more complex. Man is both a social animal and a learning animal, but many learning experiences may have either thwarted or rewarded the natural curiosity of children. Nothing stimulates learning like a real task, a task which is real to the students, which is within their capacities yet stretches them fully. We need educational methods that actively engage students in learning, whatever the subject may be, that reward independent thought rather than battering them with knowledge, and that enable them to acquire certain principles and ways of setting about exploring a problem that hopefully will become habitual in their future professional lives.

Exploring the relations between time and learning also raises intriguing questions about the possibility of speeding up learning, of more effective learning over a shorter time span. For example, we need more effective and economical ways of enabling students to acquire necessary factual material, the knowledge with which to think, and quickly to relate it to significant general ideas of principles. 'Pure theory unclouded by a single fact' is as abortive as pure fact unlighted by a single theory. In Charlotte Towle's words: '. . . educational diagnosis and prognosis involve reckoning with a configuration of factors over a period of time. The time element will be shortened as we systematically attempt to understand the significance of configurations.'[1] Understanding the significance of configurations, the content and different educational devices used in teaching as they impinge on students, the extent to which they are cumulative, isolated, too much, too little, abortive or effective, the problems of relating theory and practice to each other—all these are at the heart of what we need to know.

I have spoken about problems of teaching and learning in rather impersonal terms, appearing to forget that the most potent driving force in education is the interaction between persons, whether students or teachers. Two recent but unconnected papers explore and reinforce this. One was read by Helen Perlman at the Council on Social Work Education Annual Meeting this winter.[2] The other is a study by R. W. Revans.[3] Helen Perlman bases her conclusions on extensive knowledge of the behavioural sciences, together with years of experience in teaching students in a post-graduate school of social work. Revans' findings come from a series of sentence-completion attitude tests administered to over 2,000 adolescents in Lancashire secondary schools. The exciting thing is that these two unconnected papers fit together like pieces of a jigsaw puzzle. Revans found that 'the child's perception of the professional skills of the teacher is correlated with his liking for him as a person, and the child likes as a person those teachers who seem to him to know their professional task.'[4] And, 'A child's respect for his teacher's skill is strongly correlated with the simple affection, or even love, that the teacher is able to generate'.[5] Helen

[1] Charlotte Towle, *The Learner in Education for the Professions*; The University of Chicago Press, 1954, p. 396.
[2] Helen Harris Perlman, '. . . And Gladly Teach', Council on Social Work Education, Annual Program Meeting, Salt Lake City, January, 1967.
[3] R. W. Revans, 'An Operational Research Study of the Teacher/Pupil Relationship in the School Classroom', the Organization for Economic Co-operation and Development, Paris, December, 1966, DAS/CSS/66, 355 (mimeographed).
[4] *Ibid.*, p. 57.
[5] *Ibid.*, p. 78.

Perlman sees the teacher from whom others learn in these same terms, which she identifies as power and love. The creative teacher, she says, not only possesses knowledge, has made it his own, has power to put it into action, knows his stuff, but also loves his subject, feels it is important and that it matters. As she puts it: 'All of us remember with warmth some teacher . . . because he was obviously in love with the subject he taught'.' The other love, love of the learner, includes belief in him and his potentialities and pleasure in discovering how to enable him to learn and to grow. The whole paper is a tribute to Charlotte Towle who, as she rightly says, 'loved learners as she loved learning'. But, I would add, she loved learning because it enabled her to understand better how to help the learner in education for the professions.

The power and love of the teacher are obviously neither developed nor exercised in a vacuum. Their effectiveness, their power in action, come from the mutual exchange between the teacher and the students in the particular social system of a given educational institution with its own unique climate. It is not some diffuse emotion but a close two-way communication, a relationship which keeps the teacher sensitive to the gap that can exist between what he said and what members of a group heard, together with the different impact that his teachings may have upon different individuals. It is being able to look steadily into the mirror of self-knowledge held up by students so that he may see himself as others see him and be equally well aware of his perceptions of them. It is also a constant ability to be taught by students so that he may understand better how they learn. As R. W. Revans says: 'We may one day discover that nobody ever taught anyone anything: we may find our powers are limited to providing the student with the best conditions in which he may learn for himself[2]. In short, the teacher in education for social work is probably a figment of our imagination. In reality there are only learners who happen to be at different stages and with different responsibilities and who are expressing their learning in different ways. But in the meantime there is plenty for us all to learn, and we must be perennial learners if we would gladly teach.

[1] *Op. cit.*
[2] *Op. cit.*, p. 71.

4

THE PLACE OF SCIENTIFIC METHOD IN SOCIAL WORK EDUCATION*

PETER LEONARD

A social work student in the early weeks of her training once said to me in exasperated tones, 'Why do we have to think about these hypotheses and theories—why can't we just have the plain *facts*?' This kind of demand among students arises from a difficulty which faces anyone coming to grips for the first time with the nature of scientific explanation, namely the need to re-think the previous naïve assumption that understanding the world is simply a matter of the observer getting hold of the *facts* directly. At this stage my student had not yet begun to understand that perception is the interpretation of sensory stimuli and that human beings do not have a direct uncomplicated relation to events outside themselves, but that they build up what John Rex has called 'participant theories'.[1] These usually unacknowledged 'theories' reflect the way in which the individual's experience, language, values and other cultural elements structure his perception of the world.

It is the responsibility of the social work teacher to help students to understand the nature of scientific explanation in order that they may be better able to evaluate and use the results of the social sciences in social work practice. This should lead not only to a better understanding of, for example, sociology and psychology, but also to a more scientific attitude towards social work practice itself. The purpose of this paper is to outline some of the issues involved in this task.

The social sciences are concerned essentially with systems of interaction, either *within* the individual (the field of psychology), or *between* individuals and things (including persons) outside themselves (the fields of sociology, economics, etc.). The major task of the social sciences is therefore to explain these interacting systems within the individual and between the individual and objects in the environment, and 'to ask for an explanation in science is to ask for a theory'.[2]

* *Case Reference*, Vol. XXXIII, No. 5, September, 1966.
[1] J. Rex, *Key Problems of Sociological Theory*, Routledge and Kegan Paul, 1961.
[2] H. L. Zetterberg, *On Theory and Verification in Sociology*, The Bedminster Press, 1963, p. 2.

Theories are developed by the establishment of a number of propositions which are valid in several diverse contexts, and these propositions are 'the free creations of the human intellect'[1] and do not flow *directly* from the material which is being dealt with. These propositions rest upon conventions as to how certain terms shall be used and how they shall be attached as labels to observable events. In the social sciences, the relationships between various observable events are usually expressed in terms of language and this carries with it important implications which have to be understood by anyone trying to explain human behaviour. The major implication—as the modern philosophical concern with language has shown—is that the social scientist's ideas of reality, no less than the layman's, are given to him by the language that he uses. Wittgenstein was foremost in demonstrating to us that the concepts we have determine the *form* of the experience we have of the world. He writes: 'That the world is *my* world shows itself in the fact that the limits of my language (of the only language I can understand) means the limit of *my* world'.[2] Thus all observation is in terms of a conceptual framework, and the *facts* which my student was understandably so eager to gain are, in the last analysis, sense data perceived in terms of a scheme of concepts.

An understanding of the nature of theory in social science should enable the student to cope with certain important problems which occur in training and practice. At this point I want to deal with two such problems:

1. The relationship between empirical evidence, hypotheses and speculation.
2. The problem of how to evaluate divergent theories which seek to explain the same phenomena.

The first problem centres on the need for the student to be clear about the scientific and philosophical status of the various concepts he will come across during his studies. The usefulness of scientific propositions is generally seen to be in direct relation to the degree to which they can be identified with sensory data, for in this way they can be used to predict events which can be observed. Propositions which are not related to observable events cannot be tested empirically and must therefore be treated with greater scepticism than those which are

---

[1] R. C. Sheldon, 'Some Observations on Theory in Social Science', *Toward a General Theory of Action*, T. Parsons and E. Shils (Eds.), Harper, 1962, pp. 30–44.
[2] L. Wittgenstein, *Tractatus Logico-Philosophicus.* 1923, quoted by P. Winch, *The Idea of a Social Science*, Routledge and Kegan Paul, 1958.

open to such testing. Karl Popper[1] contends that in both the natural and the social sciences adherence to the method of offering deductive causal explanations and then testing them (the method of hypothesis) is essential. From the hypothesis to be tested we deduce some prediction and then challenge it by experiment, comparison, further observation, etc. Agreement between the prediction and the test we take as corroboration of the hypothesis, while clear disagreement will be seen as disproving it. Thus hypotheses are selected by a process of the elimination of the unfit. 'In order to make the method of selection by elimination work' writes Popper in a characteristic passage, 'and to ensure that only the fittest theories survive, their struggle for life must be made severe for them'.[2]

The means by which we *arrive* at hypotheses, whether by intuition, observation or sheer prejudice, is of minor importance scientifically; the important question concerns the *testing* of the hypothesis. The social work student who is reasonably clear about this is equipped with a frame of reference within which to examine explanatory statements in the social sciences. Some of the theories he comes across, such as those of psychoanalysis and Marxism, will be seen as important imaginative speculations from which some testable hypotheses may be derived. Some speculative concepts appear to hold out little hope of empirical testing, and many psychoanalytic concepts are of this kind, but they may still be valued because they appear to extend the perceptual field of the social worker. Other theories will be seen as providing a base from which numerous hypotheses can be derived which are open to rigorous testing, and from a scientific point of view these will be looked upon with particular favour. However, the social work student will not be seeking for final proof in science for, in an empirical science by definition, no propositions are exempt from empirical control and therefore no *final* truths can be established. The student will not consequently be asking, of a statement which purports to be scientific, 'Is it true?' for truth is a metaphysical pursuit; rather the student will ask of such a statement 'What is the *evidence*?'

For the social work student this empirical approach is of special importance for he will have, as a practitioner, the task of selecting the hypotheses upon which he will develop his social diagnosis and his plans for treatment in relation to particular clients. The empirical approach should help to guide his selection of hypotheses, for he will ask of himself during his work with a client, 'What is the actual

[1] K. Popper, *The Poverty of Historicism*, Routledge and Kegan Paul, 1957.
[2] K. Popper, *op. cit.*, p. 134.

evidence for my particular view of the client's problem?' His answer to this question might well reveal that a part of his view is comprised of hypotheses supported by behavioural and environmental evidence; that another part has its origin in tentative speculation, introspection and intuition, for which there is at present little supporting evidence; and that a further part has its roots in the value system and attitudes of the social worker himself. All of these elements in the social worker's view of the client's problem have their part to play in the therapeutic task. The social worker is not concerned only with causal explanations of what brings a client's behaviour about and what its consequences are; he is also attempting to acquire an interpretive understanding of the *meaning* of a piece of behaviour, to which Max Weber's term *Verstehen* applies. Weber saw this type of understanding as the hall-mark of the social sciences.

'. . . we can accomplish something which is never attainable in the natural sciences, namely the subjective understanding of the action of the component individuals'.[1]

However, this subjective understanding of one human being by another will still need to be tested against the evidence of continued observation—the social worker's intuition has always to be put to the test if possible. On this Weber remarks:

'. . . an interpretation which makes the meaning of a piece of behaviour as self-evidently obvious as you like, cannot claim *just* on that account to be the causally *valid* interpretation as well. In itself it is nothing more than a particularly plausible hypothesis'.[2]

Finally, the part of the view of the client's problem which appears to stem from the social worker's own value system and attitudes, is an essential ingredient in therapy, for as Paul Halmos[3] maintains, social work is not simply an applied science but shares with other therapies a strong moral commitment which provides the motive-force for treatment.

What social work teachers should ask of their students is that they should become increasingly adept at distinguishing various categories of statements so that value judgments may be to some degree dis-entangled from empirical evidence ('what is' distinguished from 'what

[1] M. Weber, *Theory of Social and Economic Organization*, Oxford University Press, 1947, 103.
[2] M. Weber, *Wirtschaft and Gesellschaft*, Tubingen, Mohr, 1956, in translation, by P. Winch, *op. cit.*
[3] P. Halmos, *The Faith of the Counsellors*, Constable, 1965.

ought to be') and speculation, which may be diagnostically illuminating, from hypotheses which are backed by substantial evidence. Social workers sometimes speak of the 'incorporation' of theory as the way in which theory and practice are integrated. If this means that theory becomes part of one's habitual mode of thought and that one is no longer conscious of using theoretical concepts, then it may also mean that the theory is no longer open to critical examination. In social work there has in the past been too much 'incorporation' of psychoanalytic theory and too little critical appraisal of the evidence on which the theory was based.

A reasonably clear appreciation of the nature of scientific explanation will also provide some assistance to students when presented with conflicting theories which purport to explain the same phenomena. This appreciation will enable the student to accept the inevitability of conflicting theory in the social sciences and he may come to see that ability to cope with uncertainty and even welcome it as a spur to discovery is the mark of the mature professional. The desire for absolute certainty and final truth, while understandable at the beginning of one's professional education may, if unmodified, become fossilized into a determination to hold on to theories which have gradually taken on an ideological function and are therefore impervious to empirical control.

Because the education of the social worker is directed towards social action and problem-solving, the social work teacher is committed to helping students to be 'opportunists' with respect to the theoretical concepts they use in structuring their view of particular problems. This eclectic approach demands that teachers should provide students with experience of examining divergent theories and selecting from each propositions that can be used to explain a particular problem. Arnold Rose[1] has suggested a general strategy for the examination of divergent sociological theories about the aetiology of social problems, and this strategy may, I believe, be used in social work education to examine both psychological and sociological theories in relation to particular problems. The examination of divergent theories begins by ascertaining to what extent they state the same thing using different universes of discourse. This may be done, for example, by taking a number of propositions from each of the two theories, translating them into operational terms and then matching the two sets of operational statements. The extent to which matching is possible marks the

[1] A. M. Rose, 'Theory for the Study of Social Problems', *Social Problems*, Vol. IV, No. 3, January, 1957.

degree to which propositions from the two theories are operationally identical. The next step is to examine the empirical evidence in support of those propositions derived from the two theories which are *not* operationally equivalent and tentatively accepting propositions which are supported by empirical evidence. This strategy for examining divergent theories might, in sociology, provide a means of helping students to evaluate the concepts of 'anomie' on the one hand and 'social conflict' on the other as explanations of certain types of social deviance. Likewise, in the field of personality theory, the psycho-analytic concept of 'transference' might be compared with the learning theory concept of 'stimulus-generalization', or the notion of 'identification' with that of 'modelling' or 'imitation'. By this means the student is able to discover the common assumptions which frequently underlie divergent theories and sometimes feel free to use interchangeably theoretical propositions which appear to be operationally identical.

There are two further related theoretical problems with which the student has to deal during training and after. These are:

1. The existence of a multitude of variables which appear to combine to produce specific pieces of behaviour.
2. The need, which social work practice demands of students, to use concepts and theories from two distinct frames of reference, the sociological and the psychological, and to bring them together to provide diagnostically useful explanations.

The existence of a multiplicity of causal factors for any particular piece of social behaviour means that the student is able to see that any one-factor theory about the social problems he meets may be dismissed as an over-simplification from the start. In the field of criminology, for example, neither crime in general nor any specific crime can ever be due to one single factor which would invariably produce this result. Thus, in recent years, theories of multiple causation have been developed to account for crime and single factor theories have been generally discarded. Such multiple causation theories are by their very nature eclectic and for this reason especially attractive and useful to the social worker; however, they present us with certain difficulties when we attempt to measure them against Popper's insistence on the scientific necessity of disprovable hypotheses. Leslie Wilkins[1] has suggested that multiple causation theory 'can hardly be dignified by the term theory' because it 'does not facilitate the deduction of any hypotheses or practical consequences that are of any help whatsoever',

[1] L. Wilkins, *Social Deviance*, Tavistock Press, 1964.

and it is 'at best an anti-theory which proposes that no theory can be formed regarding crime'. Herman Mannheim's answer to this[1] is to suggest that all we can do is to test one factor after another and admit that multiple causation theory, though unsatisfactory, is the best we have for it reflects 'how utterly complicated and confusing the search for the causes of crime still is'. These comments apply equally to the other kinds of human problems with which the social worker is concerned; complexity and confusion face him at every turn and he may long for the relative security of single factor theories which offer over-simplified explanations.

Perhaps the greatest intellectual challenge to the social worker, and consequently to the student and teacher of social work, is the imperative need for a psycho-social approach to human problems. This requires the social worker to integrate, in some way, biological, psychological and sociological approaches to man, to use several frames of reference in a way that scholars in the academic disciplines would find difficult and perhaps even offensive to the 'purity' of their disciplines. This multidimensional and interdisciplinary approach demands a lot of both student and teacher, and has its dangers, but provides social work with an opportunity to assist in work towards the theoretical integration of the social sciences.

Students may be helped to meet this challenge by giving attention once more to the nature of scientific explanation. From this they will see that any given piece of behaviour is inherently neither 'psychological' nor 'sociological' and that the same event may be both, depending on the body of theoretical concepts within which it is interpreted. They will see that an outburst of aggression, for example, may be 'psychological' in the sense that it may give rise both to feelings of guilt in the individual and to changes in his behaviour as a result of these guilt feelings. The same outburst of aggression may also be 'sociological' in so far as it has repercussions on family relationships. What social workers do is to move from one frame of reference to another and back again, depending on which aspect of behaviour or situation they wish to consider.

It is because students need to be able to move easily between the different frames of reference that leads social work teachers to give special attention to those theoretical concepts which appear to facilitate this movement. Thus emphasis may be placed on ego adaptability in psychoanalysis and its relationship to role theory in sociology; or attention drawn to the concept of 'reinforcement' in learning theory

[1] H. Mannheim, *Comparative Criminology*, Vol. I, Routledge and Kegan Paul, 1965.

and its relationship to the idea of 'social control' in sociology. The danger which students face here is that they may fail to keep the frames of reference analytically distinct and find themselves engaging in the kind of reductionism which explains all social phenomena in terms of individual personality, ignoring the structural elements, or which sees personality development exclusively in terms of cultural conditioning, ignoring the biological drives.

The difficulties in social work of using several frames of reference may be eased in the future if there develops a common language and a shared body of theoretical concepts used by the various social science disciplines. Personally, I find the work of Talcott Parsons, in spite of its long-windedness and occasional incomprehensibility, of particular value here. Parsons and his colleagues within their 'general theory of action'[1] have developed a framework of concepts which cover the fields of anthropology, sociology and psychology; a scheme of classification and description which aims, though hardly as yet succeeds, to provide for the social sciences what Linnaeus provided for biology in the eighteenth century. Parsons, as a sociologist, is specially interested in Freud's central contribution to an understanding of the socialization process in childhood. Parsons' examination, within his particular framework of concepts, of Freud's concept of identification[2] is an interesting example of what may be gained from using a common body of terms which can be used at both psychological and sociological levels of analysis.

In this paper, I have paid attention to some of the theoretical issues raised in teaching social work students. These issues themselves raise further practical questions about teaching methods and educational objectives. The *way* in which these theoretical issues are tackled by the social work teacher must naturally depend upon the intellectual level of the student and the resources and objectives of particular social work courses. Apart from this, however, there is a major issue facing a profession such as social work which aims to place science at the service of therapy. Social work is based upon commitment as well as science and directed towards social action rather than the gaining of knowledge for its own sake. This is just as well for, as Robert MacIver once wrote, 'science is no ready reckoner. It never offers immediate solutions to the problems of living'.[3] Consequently, the social worker, in

---

[1] T. Parsons and E. Shils, (Eds.), *Toward a General Theory of Action*, Harper, 1962.
[2] T. Parsons, 'Social Structure and the Development of Personality', *Personality and Social Systems*. N. J. Smelser and W. T. Smelser (Eds.), Wiley, 1963.
[3] R. MacIver, *The Contribution of Sociology to Social Work*, University of Columbia Press, 1931.

his day-to-day job faces two sometimes contradictory demands. If he wishes to build his work on a scientific base he must remain relatively detached and objective, sceptical of speculation, enquiring about evidence and aware that the hypotheses he is using may prove unfounded. At the same time, as a *therapist* he must, in order to sustain himself and his client, have a strong *belief* in the validity of his work, even though it is without empirical support; he must, as it were, 'suspend belief', act upon intuition and 'hunches', and have, at least occasionally, a degree of emotional investment in his relationship with the client which makes scientific detachment impossible. Although social work has developed various mechanisms, such as supervision, consultation and case discussion, which aim to bring together therapeutic investment and scientific objectivity, the tension between these two elements in social work is unlikely to be eliminated. Perhaps this is what makes social work such a stimulating but difficult job.

5

A SOCIAL WORK APPROACH TO COURSES IN GROWTH AND BEHAVIOUR*

CHARLOTTE TOWLE

In the education of social workers, knowledge and understanding of human behaviour has central importance. Inevitably, courses in human growth and behaviour have been a perennial problem. Among them the courses in normal behaviour, that indicator of growth and development, have presented greater difficulty than those in psychopathology. I will identify only two problems which have concerned the faculty of the School of Social Service Administration and describe sketchily the means by which during the past three years we have attempted to solve them through a newly designed course in growth and development of the personality.[1]

One problem has been the propensity to think in terms of absolutes —this individual is sick or well, normal or abnormal, in personality functioning. This course has a threefold aim in relation to this dichotomy.

A first aim has been that the student should see that every normal human being has the potential for becoming pathological. Every man has his Achilles' heel, every man a threshold for endurance of stress. Therefore, the stress to which he is reacting normally today, if prolonged, may be internalized tomorrow and result in abnormal responses. The individual who merely has a social problem today may become a social problem tomorrow. Time is of the essence. We emphasize the importance of prompt attention to social stresses which are causing the individual or group to function below par or in problematic ways.

A second aim has been that the student should learn that many an individual whose behaviour could be assessed as pathological still has an ego potential which may enable him to use nurturing relationships

* The Social Service Review, Vol. XXXIV, No. 4, December, 1960.
[1] The 22 weekly lecture sessions and 11 biweekly discussion sessions of 1–1/2 hours' duration extend over the first two quarters of the first year are required of all students. The lectures have been given by the same casework instructor. Discussion sections have been led by other members of the casework faculty.

and opportunities to mitigate the disease process so that his functioning is improved. We insistently teach the student to assume that the individual has a potential for recovery until he has shown otherwise by his responses to our own helping efforts and the efforts of others, or by the psychiatrist's appraisal.

Since social workers serve man only under stress of a sufficiently disabling degree that he seeks or is referred for help, it is our third aim that the student should learn that, although behaviour under stress may resemble pathological behaviour, disturbed behaviour does not necessarily connote pathology of the personality. The social worker needs knowledge as a basis for appraising stresses and perceiving the import of the adaptations and defences that the individual uses in coping with stress. He needs to know that anxiety produced by stress may motivate learning, goal-striving and problem-solving, and that it may also impede or cause a breakdown in motivation and capacity to use opportunities for learning and problem-solving. Thus students must learn that adaptations and defences may bespeak either potentials of the ego or failures of the ego. The adaptations and defences by which everyone throughout life maintains equilibrium under stress, masters obstacles, and thus gets his needs and wants met so that he is nurtured for growth bespeak the wisdom of the organism.

In teaching normal human behaviour, one focuses sharply on the interrelated wisdom of the body and the wisdom of the psyche. In the health and disease course taken concurrently, students are introduced to Cannon's principle of homeostasis; in this course in human growth and development they are introduced to Freud's parallel principles of economy and stability, in short, to the part played by the law of equilibrium in personality growth and development at all stages of maturation.

The second problem is that the traditional course in normal human behaviour often, though not always, has failed to meet the need of the social worker, largely because it has been taught by psychiatrists rather than by social workers. Criteria for differentiating normal ego functioning under stress from ego dysfunctioning characteristic of pathology frequently have been lacking. When the psychiatrist has taught normal behaviour, he often, but not always, has depicted personality as it conceivably would develop under beneficent circumstances. To show the significance of nurture he has depicted, through citation of pathological cases, what happens when nurture is lacking. The blueprint of maximum development at a given maturation stage is essentially that of an untroubled individual, a seemingly defenceless individual operating smoothly as he copes with a manageable reality, one in which his needs are being met and in which the demands of life are within his integrative capacity. The part that defences are playing in that smooth functioning and in that integrative capacity remains in the background, implied perhaps but not made explicit.

Students have reacted in two ways to courses taught by the psychiatrist. First, they often inappropriately see and feel their clients as fitting into the pathology blueprint more than into the normal behaviour picture, for clients inevitably are under stress, their defences are in bold relief, and in some areas of life they are unable to cope without help. Students do not readily see the ego potential and the latent strengths. From the psychiatrist's presentation of ego-superego development, students are prone to regard conscience as superego pathology rather than as a symptom of good ego development and as an essential for further growth and development as a social being. The social worker's fear of an over-developed conscience has been widespread enough to constitute a conspicuous weakness in helping individuals to integrate the pleasure and the reality principles. For example, in correctional work it has been noted that the social worker is prone to identify with the offender to such an extent that he defends him against the law rather than helping him face the consequences.

Second, the psychiatrist's delineation of mature personality provides the student with an ego ideal, a self-concept with which he identifies at least wishfully. It becomes a goal and a measuring stick by which he appraises himself. Since the picture of the theoretically mature adult is one to which the best of us at our best only approximate, the student feels his shortcomings, not to mention those of his mentors, of whom he may become more critical than of himself. Students are under stress at a stressful life period, when the external stress of heavy demands exerts pressure for inner change. At moments of ineptitude and in the process of feeling with clients in order to relate to them, students tend to identify with the client. Soon they are using the pathology elements in this course, and in later pathology courses, against themselves. In contrast, an initial pattern-setting course in human behaviour which focuses sharply on ego-functioning under stress can be drawn on by students in understanding themselves without provoking so much anxiety. It should arouse fewer defences against learning and thus facilitate movement into self-awareness. It should also result in more realistic self-appraisal. Over a period of three years, we have had clear evidence that the course in human growth and development does not eliminate anxiety about the self but that it lowers it and supports the student's ego for coping with it.

Of course not all courses in normal growth and development taught by psychiatrists have had the defects specified above. When the psychiatrist gives social workers the kind of course they need, he speaks out of his experience with social workers, hence almost as a social worker. And so we say, let us speak for ourselves. Perhaps the major reason for the growing trend towards assumption by the social work educator of responsibility for structuring and teaching in this area is our desire to solve the problem of the social worker's long-standing over-dependence on the psychiatrist. Students, generation after generation, have regarded the psychiatrist as the authority on the whole gamut of human behaviour because, with only few exceptions, the psychiatrist has been the teacher. If social work educators cannot assume responsibility for this part of the curriculum, we cannot hold our profession responsible to speak and act with the authority of knowledge which should be peculiarly ours. We have had a long and rich experience in dealing with individuals under stress. We should be able to speak with some authority on normal ego-functioning under stress and in many instances to differentiate the normal from the pathological.

What content have we selected? We have felt the need of a wider range of knowledge than has been taught in the traditional growth and development course. Having experienced the shortcomings of the typical presentation of the anatomy of the personality and dynamics of its functioning, which tended to produce man as an id, ego, superego abstract, we have wanted man to emerge less of a wraith, more as flesh and blood. We therefore have selected and woven together four areas of basic content. They are:

Ego—superego development and integration. In the selection of content, the traditional has been retained. In fact, it is basic. We teach the Freudian ego psychology concepts of personality structure and functioning. Among student materials there is a mimeographed statement, 'Ego-Superego Development and Integration and the Defence System'.[1] This material is kept at hand for study and application throughout the course. It is taught with close reference to man in his social context, and therefore, to what development is expected and to what defences are appropriate and normally prominent in each maturation stage. For example, the stages in development of conscience are given prominence. The relationships among physical and mental development, social milieu and ego development are in continuous

---

[1] Adapted from Charlotte Towle, *The Learner in Education for the Professions,* University of Chicago Press, Chicago, Illinois, 1954, Chap. 3.

focus. Psychosexual development and psychosocial development are closely interrelated. Criteria of relative maturity in each stage are presented as the individual moves from functioning largely under the pleasure principle to functioning which could be characterized as an integration of the pleasure and the reality principles. Thus the superego comes to be seen as the conveyor of the culture and culture as the reality principle. The significance of culture for ego-superego development is made explicit throughout the course. For example, some families and some cultures produce oedipal complexes, others merely oedipal conflicts. Students are acquainted with the still controversial possibility of the lack of either in some cultures, as made known currently in the writings of certain social anthropologists.

Integration of learning; behaviour dynamics in goal-striving. A second area of content has to do with the integration of learning, which involves understanding of behaviour dynamics in goal-striving. Since social work practice in helping individuals and groups to solve problems lies midway between education and therapy, and since goal-striving is a pervasive aspect of normal social functioning, it is important that a course in normal human behaviour should acquaint students with man as learner and as goal-striver. This is essential for use in understanding clients and also for making meaningful the values and behaviour of colleagues and one's self. As a frame of reference to focus the students' reading in this area, their mimeographed materials contain an abstract[1] on the significance of ego development and the purposes served by adaptive and defensive behaviour in learning. This material provides a scheme for the appraisal of each stage of life as presenting an integrative task in relation to integrative capacity. It thus helps the student envisage the conflicts and stresses of each period. In fact, it is part and parcel of the method for appraisal of growth and development that is being taught.

Maturation and acculturation expectancies: developmental norms. The skeleton structure, the anatomy and the dynamics of personality implied in these two areas become something other than abstractions only as they are clothed in a portrayal of human development. As a third area of knowledge, we draw heavily on the writings from this field, which show the physical, neurological, mental, emotional and social development which normally occurs at each stage of life. This content is related more closely to ego development and ego-functioning in goal-striving than is much of the human development literature.

The individual in society. The fourth area of content is drawn from

[1] Towle, *op. cit.*, Chap. 4.

the social sciences. This includes family organization and dynamics, the changing family and its import for personality growth and development, its controversial import also for Freudian theory which evolved through the study of individuals reared in families in which responsibility roles were rigidly defined and sexually determined, a family which perhaps is becoming a period piece. We draw also on the social anthropologists' writings which integrate the social sciences and the psychoanalytic point of view in showing the significance of culture for personality growth and development. We draw on the writings of a few theologians for the significance of religion in personality growth and development. A thread running through the entire course is the continuous speculative reference to what modern society is doing to man and to the import of personality growth and development for the society man has created and is creating. The instructor repeatedly moves from considerations of growth of the individual to the broad social implications, with the purpose of directing students to use what they are learning in appraising the current social scene.

These areas of knowledge are made meaningful through continuous use of case examples of individuals in their social context. Vignettes of individuals under stress, developed by students in response to an assignment, have been used to good advantage both in the lectures and in discussion sessions. The areas of knowledge interplay closely as we teach the following specific aspects and stages of life.

Stress. Although only one lecture is devoted to the subject of stress, attention is given to it throughout the course. Stress is defined and stresses are grouped into the universal (those which are occasioned by maturation in relation to changing social demands) and the exceptional (those which hit some and not others, or some more frequently than others to become inordinately burdensome for one set of reasons or another). In teaching stresses which, when they are beyond the individual's integrative capacity of the moment, give rise to defences, the theme is that what is stress to one individual is not to another. A stress may be one man's meat, another man's poison. The same stresses not only have different meanings to different people but have different import for the same people at different times, contingent on factors such as the value system of the individual and his group, the meaning of the stress to others in close relationship to the individual, and the inner and outer resources of the individual at the time the stress is encountered.

Timing is emphasized as a decisive factor to which students are taught to be alert in appraising the import of defences against stress.

For example, timing is considered in relation to both chronological age and maturation stage. The student considers life periods which ordinarily are stressful in terms of growth and change that is occurring. He considers also the vulnerability of specific life periods to stresses of a certain nature, for example, the loss of a parent at the height of the oedipal period, or a physical handicap which limits activity in late childhood when the nuclear conflict is 'industry versus inferiority'. One acquaints students also with the positive and negative implications of uneven development in body systems in relation to the nature and timing of the stress and of the import of stress in movement from one culture to another or in living in two cultures, particularly when they are incompatible cultures. This leads to consideration of the cumulative effect of a close sequence of stresses or of concomitant stresses. We teach that a repetitive stress, a condition encountered frequently by social workers, may or may not be profoundly traumatic, contingent on whether or not the individual mastered the original stress, learned from it, and resolved the conflicts which it engendered. Thus a repetitive stress may be coped with more adequately than an initial one. Finally, appraisal of the meaning of stress can well take into account the context of the times. For example, in the depression years the poverty-stricken had respectable company; being jobless was not necessarily the ego threat that it is at a time of full employment. Or today the segregation issue creates a climate in which the Negro in some communities is less able to deny his stressful plight. With the risk of open warfare constantly aired he may be fortified or even pushed to battle for his rights and be submitted to inordinate stress.

Adaptive and defensive behaviour. The significance for ego development of adaptive and defensive behaviour manifestations is taught heavily. These manifestations are presented in a lecture—but this difficult subject does not lend itself to a few easy lessons. We have encountered a problem because of the difficult task implied in recognizing and in appraising behaviour in these terms, and also because of the varied emphases and points of view in the literature. To help clarify confusion, the instructor has prepared a statement entitled 'Adaptive and Defensive Behaviour', which differentiates adaptation and defence more sharply and more narrowly than in much of the literature.

In teaching that the ego represents the propensity, innate and acquired, of the individual to adapt in the interest of survival, it is made clear that adaptation does not necessarily imply personality growth. Man as he functions for better or worse in society, and as he is shaped or shapes himself to meet or to defeat his ends, is a product of adaptation. The outcome of adaptation is contingent on selection. We should therefore not worship adaptation *per se*. What one adapts to is decisive for personality growth or regression. Adaptations can therefore be ego supportive, ego-building, or they can constrict or impoverish the ego. They may render it unsocial, asocial, or antisocial, contingent on the extent to which the individual's selection is not determined by a mature sense of values, a socially enlightened ethic. We look to the current scene in which many episodes are challenging our worship of adaptation as a means to survival, in the sense of maximization of the self. They challenge also a system of values in which many individuals get a concept of self as adequate in terms of materialistic gain. In short, good ego-functioning of mature adulthood in a democracy implies adaptation to social change, participation in effecting it, and resistance to it. We repeatedly look out to the world at large, to group behaviour and social trends, for a commentary on the import of individual personality development.

In teaching ego-functioning, there is a sharp focus on the kinds of defences that are appropriate to each maturation stage. For example, at adolescence, when the child is living in two worlds—childhood and adulthood—one can expect him to use the defences prominent in both periods. One therefore expects to see projection and flight in many forms as the youth protects himself from new adult demands which intermittently are too much for him. But we also increasingly should see those defences and adaptations which bespeak the development of conscience and the attempt to cope adaptively with reality, i.e., reaction formation against tabooed impulses, compensation, restitution and sublimation. In teaching the defences there is also a focus on appraising whether they are socially useful, whether they nurture the ego for growth or impoverish it. We present criteria for appraising a configuration of defences in terms of their ego implications.

The family. We put man in his social context through giving a view of the family. We open with a statement of the positive and negative aspects of family life. To man's long childhood within the family one attributes sympathy and altruism, man's capacity to feel with and like man. The intimacy of family life patterns him for sensitivity, flexibility, tenderness and individual conscience. The long experience in the give-and-take of intimate group life patterns him for community life and develops social conscience. Hence the function of the family is envisaged as threefold:

1. to pattern the child as a social being,
2. to stabilize and reinforce the adult as a social being through the assumption of marital and parental responsibility, and
3. to lay the foundation for spiritual development. (Faith, hope, charity (caritas) and social justice stem in large measure from the unconditional love which family life proffers to an extent not to be expected elsewhere and not often afforded elsewhere).

On the negative side the family is a source of problems; unfortunately the social worker at times thinks of it as the root of all evil. To interpersonal conflicts within family life there has been attributed man's propensity to pit himself against man. The complexity of man, neurophysically and psychologically, has made necessary prolonged dependency. This dependency has fostered the persistence of the child in man throughout life. It creates a nuclear conflict which often is lifelong—a conflict with several facets: union versus separation; at-oneness versus self-identity; dependence versus independence. To these dualities one attributes man's need for separate selfhood complicated by anxiety over separation. In the need for both dependence and independence, dependency-authority conflicts are rooted. The dual need for at-oneness and for self-identity creates unrest and fear of ego loss in intimate relationships with a reaction towards isolation, which is ego-threatening and ego-depleting. This discomfort may push the individual towards pseudo-intimacy as a compromise of dubious value from the standpoint of the function of the family and that of the socialization of the individual. The child in man often takes the form of complex rivalries, which are more than vestiges of the rivalries with parents and siblings.

The child from a family in which he has been nurtured in ways which foster ego-superego development and integration is able to emancipate himself. Emancipation implies resolution of the conflicts to a sufficient extent that their vestiges ordinarily are not troublesome, although the conflicts may be subject to reactivation. Reactivation occurs when stressful circumstances repeat the past or when inordinate stress precipitates regression. We emphasize the ego-development potentials in experiencing and resolving the normal conflicts of family life. These conflicts constitute preparation for the fray of life outside the family. This introduction leads to the question as to what kind of family is conducive to personality growth. In studying family patterns, we consider the concept of equilibrium as applied to the family group. Dynamics of family life taught at this point may serve also as background for group process taught elsewhere. Two classifications of family patterns are considered.

The first is the three-type classification: marriage bond, consanguineous and a mixture of the two. The relevance of the marriage bond family to a democratic society is shown. The incompatibility of the consanguineous family is portrayed. The significance of a marriage bond family which is one in name only, and which is 'psychological consanguineous' in terms of the ties of the child to a parent so that he is not free to establish a family of his own, is reflected upon. From this, it is shown through case examples that the criteria of maturity vary from culture to culture.

The second classification presented is the grouping of families according to responsibility roles. This has been a traditional focus in social work, one lost in the shuffle in recent years, but currently being revived. It is useful for social work's purposes in that, in helping people in problem-solving, there has been immediate relevance in knowing family responsibility roles, in order that we may use them and not undermine them, so as to work 'with the grain' of the family rather than against it. Furthermore, this classification cuts across all cultures, granted that certain responsibility alignments have higher incidence in some cultures than in others. The instructor elaborates a general classification of four types of family.[1] Each of these is considered for its potentials in fulfilling the function of the family. The family in which parental responsibilities are carried jointly and where these roles are not sharply differentiated by sex is held to be the one constituted to prepare individuals for the democratic way of life in a society which has moved towards equality of the sexes. Nevertheless, those families in which responsibility roles are more sharply differentiated and in which one parent or the other is the head of the family may also have stability, contingent on whether the needs of both parents are being met rather than violated in their relationships with one another and with the children. As parental need is met so that parents individually and jointly can meet the needs of children the family can fulfil its socializing function.

It is made clear that some disequilibrium in family life is normal. In any family in which the changing needs of the members are being met, in which the members are growing and attaining self-identity while participating in the life of the group, there will be individual and

---

[1] Towle, *Common Human Needs* (Public Assistance Report No. 8 (Washington, D.C.: Government Printing Office, 1945), re-published by American Association of Social Workers, 1952), pp. 80–94.

collective disequilibrium. We come, therefore, to this view of equilibrium in normal family life—the organization of the whole and the nature of the relationships will be such that the group resiliently can contain imbalance without suffering disintegration or distortion. Social workers encounter families at times when there is disequilibrium of a problematic kind and degree. Criteria are taught for the consideration of the family in terms of its dynamics in order to give help which lowers disequilibrium or restores equilibrium.

The point of view that no one family pattern is *the* family pattern is accepted with reservations by many individuals in the behavioural sciences. They are concerned that changes in family life are bringing confusion in sex identity and in social roles to produce profound personality problems, among them unresolved authority-dependency conflicts and anomalies in psychosexual development. Some of the specific controversies are made known. In this connection we compare the Freudian family with the modern family, leaving many questions unanswered, but asking students to observe family life with these in mind. There is some reflection upon what changes in parental roles are doing to the oedipal conflict, notably in terms of the resolution of the conflict or the lowering of it. The positive and negative implications of this conflict are envisaged. When an oedipal complex does not develop, the significance of the oedipal conflict as a civilizing force promoting sexual identity, conscience development, and more mature functioning under the reality principle leads to the question as to whether the modern family may not be lowering this conflict dangerously. Students are left with the tentative assumption that perhaps as the Freudian or Victorian family failed the child it tended to produce neuroses, whereas the modern family in failing the child perhaps produces infantile characters.

We touch on the significance of sibling relationships as a prototype of colleague relationships and therefore on the social import of resolution of sibling conflicts. It is held that sibling rivalry is universal, that statements to the contrary are suspect.

Erikson holds it to be one of the most prominent remnants of infantilism in adults.[1] It pits man against man and prompts man to outdo and outwit himself. It has been a vital force in producing this 'Age of Unreason'. When sublimated, i.e., rendered beneficent, it is a positive motivating force to which one can attribute in part the works of man which have served the common good. It is desirable that it be rendered beneficent within the family. This is not always possible

[1] Erik Erikson, *Childhood and Society* (New York, W. W. Norton, 1950).

because of defences against it. But it may occur through siblings identifying with one another. This solution may nurture the ego. It may render the child less dependent on parents and fortify him to cope with the discomfort entailed in their demands. When rivalry is expressed rather than inhibited, is understood and coped with through the meeting of need and the reconciling of conflicts, it constitutes part of the child's preparation for the healthy competition of life, a means to ego development, and a test of it. In malignant form sibling rivalry is ego-distorting. When it lends itself to management, to regulation, to sublimation, the process of self-mastery involved is ego-building. This points to the importance of dealing with sibling and peer rivalry, not stamping it under because it is taboo, or laughing it off because it is normal, but facing it and helping children to cope with it at home and at school.

We make known the fact that every child in the same family will have a different environment. This is because the family stage is set differently for each child and also because each child is unique genetically. Therefore a different environment is shaped, first, by what the child makes of it in terms of his endowment and, second, by what he means to the parents and others individually and jointly—therefore, by what he does to the life of the group. Specific determinants of environmental difference are covered. Finally, the place and function of the family is recapitulated as each stage of maturation is studied. Its relationship to the part played by school, by play, and by work is shown. The potentials of experiences outside the home, to correct, mitigate and support the effects of the family in personality development, are made known.

Methods of appraisal of growth and development. Our dual aim is to teach, not only what to look for in appraising growth and development, but also a method for so doing. This is demonstrated in the way we proceed through the study of each life period.

At the start maturation, growth and development are defined and differentiated. Maturation bespeaks the nature of man. It is the predestined change to which the organism is subject by reason of its species, the physical, neurological and cerebral changes which occur relatively independent of the environment. It is the inner change which makes for outer change in terms of behaviour. Significant for us in maturation is the fact that each phase of biological maturation is characterized by well-defined psychological attitudes. Therefore at a certain time certain behaviour can be expected.

For example, when teeth erupt there is an urge to use the new

F

equipment and the child aggresively bites—food, people, things. When the sexual glands develop the child has an urge to mate, and it is only as social reality principles have inhibited the acting-out that he delays and sublimates this impulse. In the 'terrible two'-year-old when the child walks with the uncertain certainty of the toddler, and again in adolescence, his behaviour is marked by overcertainty and indecision. In the latter stage, it is on a psychosocial basis in a society which does not accept the immediate use of his psychosexual development or other emerging powers. At two, the ambivalent assertion and uncertainty has a neurological basis as well as a psychosocial one.

Thus the student is schooled to know what behaviour to expect as implicit in the maturation stage modified by the development of environmentally conditioned abilities. Thus development refers to the interaction between maturational processes and environmental influence which together lead to the development of abilities and to the modification of the innate behaviour characteristic of the period in accordance with social values and demands. Growth is the consolidation of maturation and development, the integration of specific abilities, hence of progress in more effective functioning. Thus we say the child has grown in his ability to walk, talk, perceive, think and relate to people. His growth thus may be in ability to express himself through adaptation to social demands.

This triad, maturation, development and growth, have one common denominator—change; and change in human behaviour is two-directional, progressive and regressive. The student comes to know that, as environment supports maturation and socializes its psychological traits, progression occurs. In the interplay of this triad with the potentials for the configuration to promote growth or regression there is a focus on the controversial question of whether in the timing of expectations and demands it is well to anticipate the maturation stage or support it through moving at its tempo. Considerable thought is given to the tempo of demands as we proceed through the maturation stages, because of its timeliness in the current scene when the maturation push seems to be pervasive. Cultural differences and their effects are considered, to establish the significance of a society's demands on individuals in determining the tempo and the sequence of maturation push, support or lag. For the American scene, however, in the light of current trends and social problems, we arrive at the wisdom of not overpushing the maturation stage. One often defeats one's aims in so doing to produce pseudo-maturity or even regression.

We arrive also at the wisdom of not lagging behind it in affording opportunities to develop potential abilities at a time of biological and psychological readiness. In short, there is recognition that there is a time to strike while the iron is hot in the interest of maximum growth and development.

For example, for the development of capacity for relationship the crucial time for a child to receive steadfast concern and love, manifested in responses to his overtures, is in the initial pattern-setting days when he is first relating to people. Late childhood is a decisive time for the acquisition of knowledge and skills for use in sublimating the sexual impulses in adolescence and as preparation for the work interests of adolescence. Adolescence is the decisive time in which to help the child think and plan for the future as a means to stabilize him in the acculturation stress of moving from childhood to adulthood.

Many examples of overpush and lag are given. There is consideration also of the effect of cultural discrepancies on personality growth. Many indicators of discrepancies in the American scene are noted. There is speculation as to the significance of 'togetherness', of going steady, of early marriage, and of other relationship trends. May these be indicative of a defence against precocious and precarious maturation? Or perhaps the accelerated physical growth of children today, coupled with opportunities and a sophisticated way of life, makes for psychological characteristics and the development of abilities which bespeak genuine maturation and earlier stability in relationships. Only time will tell, but one tentatively assumes that, while this may be true of some, it is not true of all and that the modern tempo and style of life push beyond their capacity and so produce much pseudo-maturity. Some of the evidence to support this assumption is noted.

The design which constitutes a method for appraising growth and development may be summarized as follows:

With each maturation stage we delineate the integrative task of the period.

> The biological changes and their psychological traits which make for needs peculiar to the period which must be met for growth and development, needs which create stress pending fulfilment.
> The common expectancies and demands which confront the individual in family and community and notably in widening relationship demand. Discrepancies in timing in relation to maturational readiness and innate capacity; discrepancies in opportunity and in training to make for push or lag.

We delineate also the integrative capacity of the period.

The abilities which normally emerge as needs are met. The part played by intellectual endowment, physical and energy endowment in ego development and personality functioning.

The part played by social circumstances which support maturation and foster development of abilities.

Because some discrepancy between task and capacity usually occurs, we specify the nuclear conflict of the period, the inevitable growing pains of the period. In defining the nuclear conflict we draw on and elaborate Erik Erikson's formulations.[1] We teach the decisive importance of resolution of the conflict if the individual is to move into the next maturation stage with readiness to meet its demands. We teach also the ego supportive experiences, opportunities and measures essential for the resolution of the conflict implicit to each stage of life. We are in accord with Erikson in that we insistently teach that 'what is expected of a child at any time must be related to his total maturation and level of ego strength, which are related to his motor, cognitive, psychosexual and psychosocial stages'.[2] It is as our expectancies are realistic that the conflict implicit in growth is lowered.

In this categorical presentation, qualified by variations, the student is given the wherewithal for appraising individuals in terms of where they are in relation to norms. What norms?

The ascendant needs of the period.
The common demands of the period.
The nuclear conflicts of the period.

The traits and abilities expected, and notably the ego-functioning which bespeaks normal development in the individual's responses to the ups and downs of life.

I wish I had space to share with you the evidence that some headway has been made in attaining the aims of this course. Instead I must give you an unsupported appraisal of the outcome as follows:

1. Very notably the course extends and deepens the student's understanding of man. Man is less of an abstraction, less wraithlike. It makes known that innate endowment plays a part in man's use of nurture.

2. It delineates more specifically the part played by nurture and culture in man's growth and development. Hence it should enable the student to appraise more precisely the significance of behaviour.

---

[1] *Ibid.*, pp. 219–34.
[2] Erik Erikson, 'Youth and the Life Cycle', *Children*, VII (March–April, 1960), 48.

3. With the conception that knowledge and understanding of behaviour under social stress, and skill in the use of it in helping people cope with stress, are social work's responsibility, the students have been given the means to appraise stress more precisely both as it shapes personality growth and as it tests it.

4. With the conception of adaptive and defensive behaviour as a resource of the ego rather than necessarily as evidence of its failure, the students are more perceptive of the individual's potential health. They also view themselves more freely and with less anxiety about their own responses to the many stresses implicit in social work education.

5. The more comprehensive view of man throughout the growth and decline process enables students to see more fully the sequential significance of man's social context and to perceive the potentials for modifying the relationship between the two. But this, the use of this knowledge to help individuals and groups in their social functioning, is the task of all the helping process courses.

This course makes a high intellectual and emotional demand. There are phases when the going is rough by very reason of the fact that it has engaged the students deeply. It almost inevitably does this because of the maturation stage of the student. The young adult is strongly motivated to understand himself and others for successful pursuit of personal and professional goals. This course supports the resolution of the conflict in which he often still is involved—that of intimacy versus isolation. Through deep investment of self in attaining an intimate understanding of man, the fear of intimacy is lowered to the extent that it is possible for an intellectual orientation to bring a change in feeling, thinking and doing. Educators know that there is a potential for this among educable students as the orientation becomes something more than an intellectual one by reason of its emotional import and through being put to use. Our observations of the development of students incline us to accept the concept, 'We feel as our ancestors thought; as we think so will our descendants feel'.[1] As the ancestors of our students herein lies our hope that knowledge of human behaviour will become true understanding and wisdom.

[1] Mary Boole, 'Master Keys of the Science of Notation', cited by Ethel S. Dummer in *Why I Think So: The Autobiography of a Hypothesis* Chicago: Clarke-McClary Publishing Company, n.d., p. xi.

6

THE CONTRIBUTION OF PSYCHOANALYSIS TO SOCIAL WORK EDUCATION*

WERNER W. BOEHM, D.L.

THE relationship between psychiatry and social work has been a close one for several decades during which psychiatrists have served as consultants in social agencies and as teachers in schools of social work. The ties have been mutually rewarding. In particular it is psychoanalysis, seen in its threefold aspects—as a system of theory, a method of investigation, and a method of therapy—which has had a profound impact upon social work. Psychoanalytic concepts constitute a portion of social work theory, and psychoanalytic techniques of therapy in modified form have been incorporated into the treatment system of social casework, the oldest and best developed of the methods of social work. Since this paper is focused on the contribution of psychoanalysis to social work education, my remarks will be concerned with psychoanalysis as a theoretical system. I shall not, therefore, deal with psychoanalysis as a method of investigation or as a therapeutic technique. I shall discuss its contribution from the vantage point of my three years' experience in directing the comprehensive Curriculum Study of the Council on Social Work Education.

One of the major issues with which the Curriculum Study naturally had to wrestle was clarification of the theoretical base of social work practice. This is an extremely difficult issue to deal with as long as the nature of social work itself has not been clearly defined. There is little doubt that psychoanalysis will remain one of the bodies of knowledge contributing to social work theory. There are, however, some questions as to the extent of this contribution and some problems as to the most effective ways in which it can be made. It is to these questions that this paper will be addressed.

It is in the nature of the relationship between a scientific discipline and the body of theory of a profession that only selected concepts of that discipline, rather than the discipline as a whole, contribute to the profession's body of knowledge. Hence, it is necessary to sort out those

* Published in *Social Casework*, Vol. XXXIX, No. 9, November, 1958.

concepts relevant to the profession which are used by each of the appropriate scientific disciplines. The Curriculum Study, faced with this problem of selection, developed a statement on 'The Nature of Social Work'. This statement served as a framework for the entire study and made possible also the selection of concepts relevant to social work from a variety of scientific domains, including psychoanalysis.

In the Curriculum Study social work is viewed in terms of its functions and activities and its ultimate goal. The Study seeks to underscore the evolving character of the social work profession and the changing nature of its practice as it responds to changing needs in society. Several assumptions are made. The major ones are: (1) that social work practice is an art with a scientific and value foundation; (2) that social work as a profession exists because it meets human needs and aspirations recognized by society and that, therefore, it assumes some of the social control functions of society.

The Study conceives of the goal of social work as the enhancement of social functioning wherever the need for such enhancement is either socially or individually perceived. Social functioning, in this context, designates those activities of an individual considered essential for the performance of the several roles he is expected to carry out by virtue of his membership in social groups. All role performance requires reciprocal activity or social interaction between individual and individual, individual and group, and individual and community. The professional activities whereby the goal of social work is reached can be grouped into three functions: restoration of impaired capacity, provision of individual and social resources and prevention of social dysfunctioning. Thus, professional social work focuses upon the social relationships which express the interaction between man and his social environment. Or, to put it differently, social work proceeds on the assumption that the nature of any problem in the area of social interaction has two dimensions which are interrelated; the individual's potential capacity for the performance of his social roles and the social resources available to satisfy his needs for self-fulfilment. Hence, the social worker focuses at one and the same time upon the capacity of individuals, singly and in groups, for effective interaction and upon opportunities in the social environment measured by their contribution to effective social functioning.

In essence, this definition of social work postulates that social workers have (1) a perspective and (2) a focus of activity. The perspective is a conception that views man and his environment as a field of interacting forces. This perspective social work shares with most helping professions. The focus of social work activity is the professional intervention in only that aspect of man's functioning which lies in the realm of social relationships or of social role performance. This focus on social relationships is suggested as the distinguishing characteristic of the social work profession.[1]

Activities in the area of social relationships are not, of course, the exclusive domain of social work practice, but the focus on this area is the feature that distinguishes social work from the activities of other professions whose primary concern resides in other realms. The physician, although sharing the social worker's perspective, focuses primarily upon somatic phenomena; the psychiatrist, upon emotional phenomena; the minister, upon spiritual phenomena; the teacher, upon intellectual phenomena; and so on. All of these professions realize that physical, psychic and social factors are interrelated, but their particular professional emphasis causes them to focus their professional talents on a particular aspect of man. It is our contention that, by identifying their common perspective as well as the characteristic focus of each, it is possible to perceive both the similarities and the differences of the various helping professions, of which psychiatry is one.

Clearly, such a definition of social work implies that, at the base of social work practice, there must lie concepts drawn from theories describing the individual and his endowment, the social environment and the interaction between individual and social environment. Most specifically, for effective practice social work needs to utilize theoretical concepts about man's physical and psychological functioning, concepts describing the behaviour of social groups, concepts about societal and cultural forces, and concepts about the various interrelationships. All of these contribute to our understanding of man in his social functioning. In this vast array of theoretical material, there is a place for psychoanalytic theory, specifically for those concepts which enhance the social worker's understanding of the nature of man's psychic forces put to use in the performance of his social roles. In other words, the major contribution of psychoanalysis, in the light of our definition of social work, consists of its concepts of ego psychology. It is the concepts of the ego, its functions and dynamic relationships with the other personality concepts, the id and the superego, and their linkage with the theory of sexuality and the unconscious which con-

---

[1] For a more thorough development of these points, including the underlying assumptions, the essential values, and the goal and functions of social work, see Werner W. Boehm, 'The Nature of Social Work', Social Work, Vol. III, No. 2, 1958, pp. 10–18.

stitute the core of the contribution of psychoanalysis to social work.[1]

Why do we find concepts of ego psychology particularly useful for the practice of social work? The answer lies in our conception of social work. Social work seeks to enhance social functioning. We know that social functioning is in large measure the result of the orchestration by the individual of a vast array of physical, psychic and social factors. To be able to orchestrate these factors, the individual must first of all be able to perceive them realistically. Then he must be able to relate them to each other in pertinent ways. And, lastly, he must try to find expression for them through the things he does, his activities, 'his social functioning'. Thus, it is these attributes of the individual—perception, integration, orchestration and execution—which are the functions of the ego and are utilized in the process of social functioning.

Ego psychology is a large theoretical realm. It is relatively well developed, and this fact itself may account in part at least for the somewhat heavy use of this theoretical system in social work in comparison with the utilization of social theory. Indeed, theories of the social environment are less well developed. The social work educator who argues that social work practice is in need of theory, not only theory dealing with the individual but also theory dealing with society, is immediately faced with the problem of interrelating theories that are in different stages of development. In addition, he requires an integrating construct whereby concepts describing society can be linked, for only then is the social worker able in this practice to make a systematic examination of social and individual factors and their place in the creation and solution of problems. We have no answer to the problem of uneven development of theories but it is our assumption that the concept of social role provides the integrating construct because it permits the assessment of both individual and social factors and their relationship.

The utilization of ego psychology concepts in social work presents a number of problems, both for the social work educator and for the psychiatrist who may serve as a teacher in a school of social work. These problems, related to psychoanalysis as a theoretical system, may stem from differences in philosophic outlook, may be related to the dynamic character of ego psychology, or may be caused by differences in the respective goals of social work and psychoanalytic practice.

There are a number of secondary problems which have to do with

---

[1] Annette Garrett, 'Modern Casework: The Contributions of Ego Psychology', in *Ego Psychology and Dynamic Casework*, Howard J. Parad (ed.), Family Service Association of America, New York, 1958, pp. 38–52. This chapter contains a thorough and able description of the concepts of ego psychology applicable to social casework.

the fact that it is not always easy to distinguish between psychoanalysis as a system of theory, a method of investigation, and a method of treatment, and that in some respects there is a certain similarity between the practice of psychoanalysis and that of social casework. These problems are clearly outside the focus of this paper and will, therefore, not be dealt with. Nor shall I deal with the problem of the social worker's possible loss of identity as a result of his close association with members of a higher status profession, which utilizes a somewhat similar theory. I consider these problems as secondary because I believe that, as social work and psychiatry continue to clarify their distinguishing characteristics, they will be in a better position to identify their similarities and differences. Thereby, the relationship between the two professions will become clearer. More exchange of theory between the two fields should take place when it is recognized that social work, from its knowledge of social situational factors affecting the lives of clients and patients,[1] has specific theoretical contributions to make to psychiatric practice.

1. *Philosophical Differences between Psychoanalysis and Social Work*

Social workers and psychiatrists may hold different views about various aspects of the socialization process. First of all, social workers may question whether psychic forces are to be considered as forces that are inherent in the person's constitution, only to be moulded or 'tamed' in the crucial socialization period of the early years of life when the child interacts with the important members of his immediate family. Such a view, which is now also being challenged by some psychiatrists and behavioural scientists, does not preclude consideration of social factors as impinging upon the etiology of neuroses. But it does mean that social factors are seen as secondary forces not as possible codeterminants. Obviously, the question cannot be answered in the absence of research findings, but it should be raised.

Another related aspect of the socialization process about which there may be a difference in point of view is the assumption often made by orthodox Freudians that the ground work for the possible outbreak of neurosis in the future is laid in the first few years of life when the character structure of the individual is determined. Kubie, a proponent of this point of view, refers to this as the 'creation of the neurotic potential'. Whether or not the 'neurotic potential' gets transformed into 'neurotic process' and ultimately eventuates in a 'neurotic state'

[1] Heinz Kohut, M.D., discussion of Annette Garrett's paper, 'Modern Casework: the Contributions of Ego Psychology', unpublished. This point is stressed several times in this excellent paper.

depends on the impact of life events and circumstances, hence, the impact of social factors.[1]

According to this view, social factors are related much less to the etiology of neuroses than to the form of their expression and their prevalence in different socio-economic groups. The position set forth in our definition of social work would raise some question about this assumption. It would argue that possibly the primary socialization process goes beyond the first five years of life and extends into late adolescence, or even early adulthood, and that social factors may have a crucial impact, not only upon the form and prevalence of neuroses, but possibly also upon their etiology. Be that as it may, even in the absence of an answer, the raising of the question could lead to a more careful delineation of social factors as possible determinants of neurotic behaviour, and to a less deterministic point of view about the inevitable predominance of psychic factors either in the etiology or the symptomatology of neuroses.

Behind these two questions lies a more fundamental one: What is the interrelationship between social and individual factors; what do we know of their identity, combination, intensity and accessibility to professional intervention? This question seems to raise a central theoretical problem, not only in social work but also in psychiatry. In fact, it constitutes the major issue in the theory of social psychiatry and social psychology. Social work, by virtue of its practice, cannot help being concerned with the effective functioning of individuals. Therefore, in the absence of tested theory, it needs a pragmatic theoretical approach to this interrelationship. It will be ready to abandon its pragmatism only when a greater degree of scientific certainty has been achieved. In the meantime it seeks to contribute to this end out of its own experience and wisdom.

Let us grant, for the time being, the validity of the view that man's psychic characteristics are given and universal. Social work would like to raise the question whether their interplay with the social environment cannot be better understood by differentiating among the variables which constitute the rather vague entity 'social environment'. Which variables at different points in the life cycle have an immediate and direct impact upon the individual? Which, since they are of a more general character, have only an indirect impact and cause only mild repercussions on the lives of the actors on the family stage? For

[1] See Lawrence S. Kubie, 'Social Forces and the Neurotic Process', in *Explorations in Social Psychiatry*, Alexander H. Leighton, John A. Clausen, and Robert N. Wilson (eds.), Basic Books, New York, 1957.

instance, during the so-called formative years, which in our civilization seem to stretch into early adulthood, the development of the child seems to be influenced heavily by familial interrelationships. Hence, the patterns of love and work as acted out in the family arena constitute the major social variables to be considered. Such larger social variables as urban-rural structure, ethnic background, value systems, socioeconomic status, and the like would also need consideration. Yet they would warrant examination, not as primary forces in the interaction among the members of the family, but as possible contributing factors to the process and structure of social interaction in the family. I believe it is the complex of variables within the family unit which social workers frequently refer to as 'the social situation'.

At a later point in the individual's life, when he abandons the roles of child, sibling, student, part-time wage earner and so forth, to assume adult roles such as spouse, parent, employee, citizen and the like, the larger social variables take on importance as possible primary factors in his social role performance as an individual. By the time he is an adult, these social variables directly impinge upon the way the themes of love and work are played by him. These will now have to be considered along with the most intimate aspects of 'the social situation'. Should such a view prove to be sound, it would make possible the examination and treatment, through the methods of casework and group work, of the more intimate relationships between psychic and social factors in the family interaction. At the same time there would be a greater awareness of the impact of the larger variables of the social structure upon individual functioning, and the way would be paved for a direct attack upon those which could be dealt with through community organization and administration.

The adoption of the point of view that the larger social variables and individual psychic factors interact can lead to the elimination of the depth dimension in personality theory, the profound contribution by Freud to the understanding of personality in dynamic terms.[1] Neo-

---

[1] Herbert Marcuse, *Eros and Civilization*, The Beacon Press, Boston, Mass., 1955. See particularly the Epilogue, 'Critique of Neo-Freudian Revisionism'. Marcuse argues that the elimination of the depth dimension (libido theory) by the Neo-Freudians has led to advocacy in their psychotherapeutic practice of the ethical norms prevailing in society, minimized the depth of the conflict between man and society and contributed to the development of goals of psychotherapy which either equate mental health with 'adjustive success' or postulate such goals as 'the optimal development of a person's potentialities and the realization of his individuality' (p. 258), goals which tend to deny the reality aspects, social and individual, which stand in the way of their achievement. In this context, see also Allen Wheelis, *The Quest for Identity*, W. W. Norton and Company, New York, 1958, especially Chapter VI, 'Values'. The author argues that psychoanalytic treatment has no specific goal; it can only try to help individuals to achieve a direction, obtain control over irrationality, and chart a course.

Freudians sometimes tend to disregard the power of the unconscious and the theory of sexuality. Thereby, it becomes possible for them to develop a rather superficial and naively optimistic view of man in relation to society. This position can lead them to dispense psychological nostrums and to adopt a shallow view of life and the social demands made upon man. The social work profession, although not always as clear on this issue as it should be, would seem to reject the position that makes mental health synonymous with adjustment and is in disagreement with a therapeutic goal that encourages individuals to accept society uncritically. Rather its efforts are directed towards helping people to perceive society in all of its aspects, positive and negative, and enabling them to work towards social change where this is needed. Social work takes the view that the individual must be helped to find a measure, *his* measure, of individual and social fulfilment in social functioning by dealing with problems that are intrinsic, that reside in social forces, or that stem from a combination of the two. Thus the road is left open for social criticism and social change, on the one hand, and for individual change through modifications of the psychic factors, on the other. What is needed for social work, then, is not the elimination of the depth aspect of orthodox Freudian psychology, but rather the development of an understanding of social forces in depth and a view in dynamic terms of the conflict between man and society. The absence of the depth dimension in much of the social theory at the present time is no reason to abandon the dynamic understanding of man.

2. *The Dynamic Character of Ego Psychology*

Since ego psychology constitutes the core of the contribution of psychoanalysis to social work education, it is necessary to teach it in its dynamic aspects, hence, to show the relationship of the ego concept to the concepts of the psychogenetic development of man. When it is taught in this way, the student can become aware that ego psychology is neither opposed to nor tantamount to the study of conscious processes. Further, the social work student will realize that ego psychology is not simpler than libido psychology.[1] Rather, ego psychology embodies Freudian concepts organized in such a way that the ego becomes the central concept; the ego is understood in all of its manifestations and its modes of dealing with both social reality and the internal impulses. Thus, ego psychology is obviously useful to the social worker who intervenes in social relationships. However, I

[1] This point has been well made in Garrett, *op. cit.*

believe that an emphasis on ego psychology may create a burden for the psychoanalyst who teaches its concepts. He must have a clear understanding of the social work point of view in order to select the appropriate concepts and organize them in such a way that they are presented in their proper relationship to social work practice. Some psychoanalysts have held, perhaps facetiously, that occasionally social workers possess more knowledge of ego psychology than do psychiatrists. Some have even advocated that these concepts be taught by social workers rather than psychiatrists. Be that as it may, I believe that the teaching of psychoanalytic concepts is the proper province of the psychiatrist and not of the social worker for the simple reason that ego psychology, which is a developing field, lies properly within the theoretical domain of the psychiatrist. It is he who is best qualified to cultivate his own vineyard, as it were. The social worker has to devote his energies to cultivating another vineyard, namely, the integration of theories from a variety of scientific domains and their application to problems of social work practice.

A heavy burden is placed upon the psychiatrist who becomes a teacher in a school of social work. He needs to have a philosophic orientation towards psychoanalysis in keeping with the depth view of the orthodox Freudian position, coupled with an acceptance of the point of view of social work and its emphasis upon social functioning. In addition, he should possess interest in and profound knowledge of the expanding domain of ego psychology so that he can be in a position to teach this area of theory in relation to the other aspects of Freudian theory. Such an orientation has implications for the teaching of psychopathology. It would seem that psychopathology would then not be taught in terms of symptoms of the major disorders. Instead, it would be taught conceptually. The concepts of perception and integration as functions of the ego and genetic theory would be used by the teacher to show how the inappropriate or uneconomic use of mechanisms of defence and faulty psychogenetic development of the individual can lead to psychic dysfunctioning.

3. *Limitations of Psychoanalytic Knowledge*

In order to be an effective teacher, the psychiatrist-teacher must also be aware of the limitations of psychoanalytic knowledge. The fact that social theory is underdeveloped has tended to cause some psychiatrists as well as social workers to be cavalier about the necessity of having a theoretical understanding of social factors. Socio-cultural phenomena, which often are extremely complex and difficult to understand, have sometimes been neglected or oversimplified because of the lack of theory about their impact on the individual. It would appear to be the sounder and wiser course to acknowledge theoretical limitations, in the person who teaches, in the field of knowledge as a whole, or in both than to assume that psychoanalytic concepts can actually explain the nature of socio-cultural phenomena, and their impact upon human behaviour.

4. Limitations of the Holistic View

The holistic view of man, which sees soma and psyche as inter-twined, does not always include also the interrelationship of social and endowment factors. Even when the more comprehensive view is held, it cannot take the place of understanding the parts, although it does provide a desirable perspective. We need theory of soma, theory of psyche, and theory of social forces in order to understand the parts of the configuration; we also need a theory of the configuration itself. Obviously, this is a task that will require the ingenuity of a score of scholars from many fields for decades and more to come.

The behavioural sciences have tended to compartmentalize human phenomena. This fragmented approach, while necessary for scientific progress, is not helpful for professional practice that is concerned with the whole human being. Theories of any one scientific field, such as psychology, sociology, anthropology and so forth, do not explain 'the total situation'; they explain only a portion of it. Social workers tend, therefore, to look askance at these scientific fields. They develop their own ad hoc theories, which reflect implicit or inferable formulations of practitioners. They do not make conscious application of an explicitly formulated system. These ad hoc formulations have the advantage of seeming to be comprehensive, that is, they explain the total personality structure and they focus on the individual as a whole. They have the disadvantage of leading practitioners to examine inadequately and even to overlook factors which have to be included in the total configuration. Thus, social work practice's ad hoc theory, by overcoming compart-mentalization, which is the characteristic weakness of the sciences, also loses the benefit of their characteristic strength, which is scientific rigour and precision about the factors that make up the total situation.

This ill can be cured by making explicit the practice theory formula-tions no matter how ad hoc and pragmatic they may be. Explication makes it possible to see whether a piece of theory from one of the behavioural sciences 'fits better' or adds precision. Explicit statements of ad hoc theory, in effect, would make possible systematic search for relevant social science theory. They would also facilitate the testing of ad hoc theories, and the development of a unitary theory of human relations would be hastened.

5. The Cultural Lag in the Utilization of Psychoanalytic Theory in Social Work

A cultural lag is manifest in the frequent assumption of many psychoanalysts that the only branch of social work that needs to use psychoanalytic theory is social casework. In actuality, the group worker, community organizer, administrator and researcher in social work also need to have a dynamic understanding of individuals if each one is to practice his method effectively. This fact has some implications for teaching, because the use by a much larger group of social workers of psychoanalytic theory further emphasizes the pertinence and applicability of concepts of ego psychology to problems of reality functioning. It also suggests the desirability of the psychiatrist-teacher's being familiar with the field of social work as a whole.

6. The Inaccurate Perception of the Nature of Social Work Practice

It is one of the characteristics of social work that the social worker practices under the auspices of a social agency. Thereby he is much more closely related to the control functions of society than is a member of a profession that usually practices independently, such as a psychiatrist. The latter, by virtue of his professional status, is, of course, also subject to the sanctions of society. However, by virtue of the character of his practice, which is frequently that of independent intrepreneur and not that of an employee, he enjoys much greater freedom from societal demands. This characteristic of social work practice which creates considerable conflict in the social work practitioner must nevertheless be recognized by him and his teachers because it exerts a strong influence on practice. The social worker cannot practice soundly unless he sees himself as both the agent and the conscience of society and helps the client recognize him in his dual role. In this role the social worker helps the client to recognize social limits as well as social possibilities, to become active in changing the social environment and to achieve for himself whatever individual and social fulfilment he can.

To sum up, in this paper I have asserted that ego psychology is the primary theoretical contribution of psychoanalysis to social work education and that concepts of ego psychology must be taught in dynamic and genetic context; otherwise, they will not be useful to the social worker. This aspect of psychoanalytic theory is only a portion of the theoretical base of social work. Social work practice also rests upon theories of somatic functioning and of social process. Like any profession, it reflects in its activities the incorporation of certain value systems. Psychoanalytic theory is not superordinate to, but on a par with, the other theoretical strands which constitute the knowledge base for social work practice. Man and society are viewed as an interactional field, and a depth dimension is needed for the understanding, not only of man, but also of social forces.

I have questioned the inevitability of neurosis as a result of this interaction, which is not the same as denying the likelihood of conflict between man and society. Unless the profession's view of the nature of social work, its focus of activity and its goal are shared by the psychiatrist-teacher, and unless he himself is conversant with the tremendous range and implications of ego theory, as well as with its special impact upon social work practice, it will not be easy for him to teach effectively. However, where such awareness exists the rewards are likely to be considerable, because insights into the social aspects of psychiatry may be afforded in return.

Throughout this chapter, I have sought to convey the tremendous complexity of these considerations and the need for a sceptical questioning approach to them. I have not delved into the implications for teaching of the close association between psychiatry and social work as fields of practice, nor have I dealt with the similarities and differences between the two fields of practice. I have, however, expressed the belief that clarification of the distinguishing characteristics of each field will make possible a more comfortable and effective interchange of theory, will clarify the role of the psychiatrist as a theorist-teacher for social workers, and will enable the social worker to assume the role of theorist-teacher for psychiatrists to the end that their understanding of the impact of the social forces upon the psychic economy of client or patient will be increased.

7

THE LECTURE AS A METHOD
IN TEACHING CASEWORK*

HELEN HARRIS PERLMAN

As textbooks roll off printing presses and as educators grow increasingly convinced of the necessity for the active exercise of the learner's mind, the lecture as a teaching method is looked upon with mounting disfavour. It is disparaged as a survival of the medieval book-poor university, as an evidence of sloth or incompetence in teaching ('If you are unprepared, lecture', goes the academic maxim), as an opiate for the student mind. Yet it continues to hold prominent place in the academic and professional classroom. Like the well-known redheaded stepchild, it is severely disapproved of, grudgingly admitted into the family circle, and used with heavy regularity for its services.

Teachers of casework have had particular aversion to the lecture as a teaching means. By virtue of their experience as case workers they have been accustomed to the interplay of mind on mind, to the necessity for intercommunication and interaction. By virtue of their psychological orientation they know that active participation on the part of the learner is a primary condition of learning. The lecture seems to violate both their custom and their conviction. Yet the voice of the lecturer is heard in the casework class, sometimes in unconscious imitation of traditional teaching, sometimes out of urgent zeal to deposit that which is known in the mind of the neophyte, sometimes with the worried admission that method has been sacrificed to the necessities of content. And sometimes with conviction that the lecture method has some valid place in teaching casework. This conviction motivates the writing of this paper.

The student of social casework is expected by way of his study and his classroom and field-work experience to come to know certain facts and theories about people in their social living and about social instruments in relation to people, to come to understand the significances and relationships among these areas of knowledge, to feel appropriately about that which is known and understood, and to act in

* Published in *The Social Service Review*, Vol. XXV, No. 3, March, 1951.

the interest of helping people out of that synthesis of knowledge, understanding and disciplined feeling which is called 'professional competence'.[1] In the course of his ongoing professional development it will be inevitable that he must develop broader and deeper knowledge and understanding and that he will need continuously to reintegrate and stabilize his emotional relationships to his professional experience. His education for practice, then, must help him to learn ways by which he can search for knowledge and understanding, organize it, test it, and use it to the benefit of his clients. To learn a way of doing—whether of dealing with an abstract idea or a concrete person or problem—one must do. This is why supervised field-work practice plays so important and prominent a part in all good professional education. This, too, is why the activity of class discussion is held to be invaluable as a teaching method. And this is why the lecture method raises a number of questions as to its usefulness in the casework classroom.

As the word 'lecture' is used today, it is a name given to a discourse by one person which may be a monotonous reading of written pages, or a sprightly spontaneous delivery of information or ideas, or a prolonged scolding, or an organized harvesting of the field of discussions. Long or short, stimulant or opiate, formal or informal, an exhortation, a demonstration, an expatiation, an interpretation—any of these nouns or adjectives may spring to mind when the word 'lecture' is said. Yet no one of them is specific to the process. Perhaps a working definition of the lecture is this: It is a process of verbal communication between one person and a group or assemblage of others (though it may be one other) where the responsibility for that communication is carried and discharged by the one. Is this fact of its being a one-way communication and a one-person responsibility a deterrent to the learning of the casework student? Or, to cast the question in more positive form, can the lecture serve the purpose of promoting student learning in the casework class? I think it can. Whether it will or not, however, depends on an appraisal of its limits and its possibilities.

In any course which aims to exercise the student in habits of pursuit and use of learning, the lecture must frankly be recognized and utilized as an auxiliary or supplementary method. It is a 'some-time thing'. It is a communication which either sows the seeds or garners the fruits of

[1] For elaborations of this too-compact statement, see Helen Harris Perlman, 'Content in Basic Social Case Work', *The Social Service Review*, March, 1947; and Charlotte Towle, 'Issues and Problems in Curriculum Development', *The Social Work Journal*, April, 1949.

discussion. Its meaningfulness to its hearers and their incorporation of its content can only be known by way of their responding communications, either written or spoken; and it is only in the intercommunication of the discussion that the lecture's content can be tested for its uses in the underpinning or provoking or correction of thinking.

Within its limits as an auxiliary method of teaching, the lecture in the casework class has a threefold purpose; it serves well to impart knowledge; to organize and pattern knowledge so that relationships and significance may be seen, which are the essence of understanding; and to interpret and illuminate knowledge which, though it may be in the student's intellectual possession, has not fully been savoured or digested.

It goes without saying that thinking, whether to one's self or out loud together with others, as in the discussion group, cannot proceed on air; it requires the stuff of knowledge for nurture. Knowledge of certain facts, events, situations, or theories must be part of the student's equipment by which to enter into fruitful discussions. That which the student can find in print and to which he can have ready access is knowledge to which he can be directed and can be expected to absorb on his own. It has no place in a lecture.[1] The factual developmental history of social casework, for example, might once have called for compilation and oral delivery by each teacher of that subject. Now such a lecture would be wasteful of time and energy of both instructor and student because it is available in published form in numerous sources. Better that the student should be active in making such knowledge his own and, having done so, should come to the classroom ready to think aloud about its import for the particular problem he needs to understand and solve.

But in the study of social casework there will be found numerous instances where the knowledge necessary for thought is not readily to be had or, when it can be found, its pursuit is uneconomical. Books on the theory and process of case work are singularly few.[2] Most of the writing that has been done in the field is in the form of fragmentary articles, dispersed within the covers of a variety of pamphlets and journals, often scattered over the years. Much of the knowledge of

---

[1] Out of the middle of the eighteenth century comes the voice of Dr Samuel Johnson: 'Lectures were once useful; but now, when all can read, and Books are so numerous, Lectures are unnecessary'. Of course, Dr Johnson himself was an inveterate lecturer, for all that he used the coffeehouse for his classroom!

[2] It is worth some speculation as to why the textbook in social casework is conspicuous by its absence. Gordon Hamilton's *Theory and Practice of Social Case Work* (Columbia University Press, New York, Second edition, 1951) is the one recent courageous effort to meet this need.

casework is still not written down at all: it may have been formulated in study committees and lost on the fugitive mimeographed sheet or formulated by practitioner and teacher and passed along by word of mouth until it has become the possession of the profession and yet is nowhere to be found in print; or it may be acted out in general practice and never have been formulated at all. And much of the knowledge from which casework practice operates is in the bodies of knowledge of other professions, and, while it may be found in print, it is often imbedded in a matrix of what are for casework purposes irrelevant considerations. It is wasteful of student time and diffusing to his focus to send him, as it were, to the mine for one nugget. Moreover, some facts or theories need to be known only in bold outline to serve temporarily as a basis for one aspect of a discussion. For all these reasons the lecture as a method of imparting knowledge has an important place in casework teaching. It may serve to provide such basic information as may not otherwise be available or accessible; to integrate and to make whole such portions of knowledge as have been culled from reading; to condense or telescope certain facts which need to be known at the time only in compact form. Such lectures perform the service of providing equipment with which the students may tackle their more important and compelling task—to *use* such knowledge in understanding, appraising and coming to some conclusion about the casework problems at hand.

A second major purpose of the lecture in the casework class is that of organizing and structuring of knowledge. Let it be said from the first that it is recognized that the test of good learning is the student's own ability to organize his knowledge: it is the poor learner who gulps down 'gobs' of fact and theory and lets them lie as undigested lumps in his mind's maw until they are spewed forth on demand; it is the good learner who selects, relates and combines single facts and then groups facts and ideas in a process of digestion and integration. Teaching aims at the development of these latter capacities in the learner, and the great validity of the discussion method is that by its process of 'shaking apart' a problem or issue, analysis of parts in the light of knowledge, and a recombination of those parts in their significant relationships the student is given a repeated experience in organizing for use what he knows. To this purpose the lecture may also serve.

The content and nature of casework learning is a peculiarly disorganizing experience to the average student. In part this is because it consciously aims at breaking up old academic patterns of learning. It asks of the student not only that he should know and think but also that he should feel and do. It asks that he become involved not alone with his mind but with the whole of himself. Because he is at once studying, observing and dealing with human beings in their living situations, because much that he learns arouses feeling about himself, because he finds that he is simultaneously affected by and affecting the persons he works with (and by that experience he becomes acutely sensitive to the persons he lives with, learns with, etc.), because he knows that he himself is being observed, appraised and helped, for all these reasons and for others which every case worker knows, many disorganizations in his learning patterns may occur. Every casework teacher and supervisor recognizes the fairly typical defences against this overwhelming experience, the clutching of a few rigid stereotyped concepts as safety spots, the flight into the clouds of speculation, or that denial that this is a subject matter than can be learned: 'everything depends on the individual case'.

Within the casework classroom the occasional lecture, set up for purposes of patterning or organizing that which the student has been learning or is about to undertake, may provide him a demonstration of ordered thinking and at least a temporary experience of security. The lecture with the purpose of organizing learning may take several forms. First among them is the lecture which sets the framework and essential structure of the course—what its scope, its bounds, its functions and its means are—in short, its essential working anatomy. Perhaps it is facetious to suggest this, but some grain of truth lies in it: that a major purpose of this lecture is to place squarely on the shoulders of the teacher the responsibility for formulating the bone and flesh of course content. When he has done this, he is ready to extract from it what will be useful to the student's beginning and continuing orientation. If the student's own efforts are to have direction and purpose, he must know—and he wants to know—what, in general, he will be expected to work at in this course, what problem areas will be covered, what focus will direct his learning effort, what responsibilities he will carry. Such a lecture, in whole or part, serves as preview or review of essential content seen within a steady frame of reference.

Classroom discussion of content, within this frame of reference, is diversified, colourful, dynamic; and because there are so many persons and problems and processes involved, there may be a tendency to fragmentation on the part of the student—he sees small pieces of everything and the whole of nothing—or he finds himself in that commonplace morass of 'loose ends hanging in mid-air'. Particularly in the cross-movement of ideas within discussion, in the pause and arrest of the student's mind as it tussles with some intractable idea or fact, in the two-way movement between case detail and general theory, disorganizations in the student's thinking may occur. A brief periodic lecture may help him to take inventory. Such a lecture purports to take stock, to come to a full stop and to answer this question: 'Where are we, in relation to where we have come from and where we are bound for?' And to answer this question: 'What is the relation of these trees to the woods, or of this woods to these trees?' Quite typically such a lecture must fill in some gaps not covered in discussion. Always it must pull together the pieces and make them part of a whole. The pieces are those examples and instances and partial explorations of meaning which case materials and discussion have yielded up; the wholes are those major concepts and principles which give significance and relatedness to phenomena which have been taken cognizance of singly. Thus, the lecture which would serve to organize knowledge must clearly identify the significant principles or theories which the base materials have exemplified or brought to life, and then the relatedness among those guiding concepts and principles. No new ideas or knowledge are put forth here. Rather, what the student has already learned and thought in small part is placed in some orderly relationship, either to other knowledge which he has or to some generalization of that knowledge. It is only as knowledge is ordered, related and generalized that it is transferable from one situation to another and made usable to its bearer.

One might fear that, if the instructor consistently takes and discharges the responsibility for filling in and pulling together and patterning the student's accumulating knowledge and experience, he will delay the development of capacity in the student himself to order and synthesize his thinking. I hasten, then, to interpolate briefly a comment or two which deserve (but cannot have here) considerable development: The lecture which organizes knowledge presents implicitly, and may well make explicit, a demonstration of a way by which that which has been perceived and thought about may be understood and used in further study. The logical outline, the relating of the general to the specific, the part to the whole, the putting-together of problems and analysing their elements of likeness and difference, the application of past learning to present problems, the identification of characteristic processes—these are among the many ways in which what is known to the student may be shuffled, selected and brought into clearer perspective and new significance for him. The student likes this; he wants it, because it is useful to him; it helps him make order out of what is often chaos for him. Most students struggle for some organizing pattern of their own when the impact of new ideas and experiences is heavy, and many take on some of the patterns demonstrated in the knowledge-organizing lecture. Whether what is taken on is taken *in* remains to be tested. Such testing takes place in the papers students are required to write, in examinations, and to some extent in class discussions. This means that written assignments and examinations and conduct of discussions must be so set up that the demand for selective, relevant analysis or synthesis is explicit. It has been my observation that out of this continuing requirement, out of his own search for order, and, in part, out of his conscious or unconscious imitation of the instructor's ways of organizing subject matter, the student develops both responsibility and a greater capacity in making his knowledge manageable for use.

Perhaps the major and the best purpose served by the lecture in the casework class is its use for interpretation. 'The general principles of any study you may learn by books at home,' wrote John Cardinal Newman, 'but the detail, the colour, the tone, the air, the life which makes it live in us, you must catch all these from those in whom it lives already'. The teacher of case work is one in whom the subject 'lives already'; he should be its most vital interpreter. The lecture for interpretation may range from the painstaking clarification of meaning to the illumination of facts and ideas by their being warmed by feeling and lighted by imagination. First, as to the need for the instructor's explaining and making clear:

In the casework reading to which students are referred and among which they browse on their own and also in the common parlance of the profession are many terms, principles and concepts which are used variously, connoting now one thing, now another. Sometimes this is a matter of semantics; sometimes it is an actual sharp difference of opinion; and sometimes the difference represents not the juxtaposition of ideas but rather the evolutionary changes in an idea. The terms 'transference' and 'relationship', for example, are encountered continuously in casework literature, sometimes interchangeably, sometimes juxtaposed. The term 'diagnosis' runs a gamut from meaning a static descriptive category of pathology to a fluid appraisal of the meaning and import of a person's behaviour in a given situation, and, likewise, a gamut of emotionalized opinion from contempt of that process to its worship. Examples could be multiplied. It is not enough for the student to be exposed to what is sometimes a difference and sometimes an actual confusion and be told to find his own way or come to his own conclusions. (Not infrequently this is done in the name of educational method when, on closer examination, it turns out to be the instructor's undue optimism or lapse of energy!) The average student has as yet neither the knowledge or experience, the breadth of view, nor the perspective by which to do so. He needs to have explained to him the whys and wherefores of these apparent inconsistencies and their relationship to the profession's own ferment and change.

This explanation is unquestionably the instructor's responsibility. He may choose to discharge it in different ways—briefly or at length, depending on considerations of relevance, importance and the students' base of preparation; he may set it as a task for the students to pursue; or he may take it as a task which temporarily, until their basic work is done, he will carry for them. But in any event he must be ready by his own clarity of position and formulation to open up and define and clarify obscurities or conflicting issues.

Beyond this plain need to make clear by definition and exposition is the need for interpretation which lights up the subject matter from within, which infuses it with qualities of feeling insight. All great teaching has this characteristic, but the humble among us recognize that greatness is not attained by will. Nevertheless, every teacher, if he is ready to be a teacher, is equipped in ways which should make it possible for him to impart some lighted vision of sweep and depth to his students. That he is a teacher of a subject matter should mean that he knows its parts and its wholeness and also that he knows the gaps and interstices between its parts and the ragged restless edges of its whole. He knows his stuff, as the students say, not at all in the sense that he is or feels completely knowledgeable or knows it cold (again an apt student way of designating fixity of knowledge!). He knows it, rather, in the sense that he has lived so intimately with this 'stuff' that it has become part of himself. And, when that has come about, he comes to be able to view it introspectively and in perspective, to examine it more closely, to turn its facets to the light of thought, and to see over, under, into and about it. Perhaps this is the salient contribution which the teacher has to make to his students—not a more exact knowledge (for, to be sure, in the casework class there are many students who may know more of this programme or that process than the teacher), or just the logical ordering of knowledge, or yet the brilliant play of ideas about it (for he may not be so gifted) but rather that 'having lived intimately with his subject, he can impart the colour, the tone, the air, the life.'

The average student does not experience these elements alone or even in communication with his fellows. He is caught up and immersed in a welter of learning experience. In his field work he is involved physically, intellectually and emotionally in experimenting with his use of his knowledge and understanding. In his classes he is in pursuit of learning in several different areas. He does well if he grasps and grapples with them and tries to make them his own. This he struggles to do in his reading and writing and class discussions. So there are times when his energies or enthusiasms must flag, his vision becomes blurred, he begins mechanically to take the word for the spirit. Every teacher knows these low spots among his students. At such times the student needs the refreshment of the teacher's understanding, perspectives and convictions. A typical example of this state is the reaction encountered in the advancing student: having nibbled lightly at the delicacies set forth in writings on psychotherapy and having chewed hard on the plain nourishment of the dark bread of casework, he begins, with lack-lustre eye, to wonder if casework really is worth doing after all. ('It doesn't reorganize the personality'. 'It doesn't deal with the basic problems.') It is at such a point that the casework teacher, equipped by having lived with the subject and experienced it affirmatively and deeply, 'believing' in it, if you will, shares his conviction, his point of view, his interpretation of the issue with the class. This, he says, is the rationale, the goal, the value and the work of your practice—let me help you to see it from another perspective.

This is the interpretive lecture, inspired, so to speak, and frankly slanted by the bias and conviction of the teacher. It will hold refreshment for the student if he has come to be identified with his teacher and if the teacher himself remains cognizant and unafraid of his bias. 'This is my belief; you may share it or let it be' or 'This is my opnion, but you may disagree strongly, along with a lot of others' expresses his attitude. It seems to me that the student not only has the right to expect that his teacher knows his subject matter and will lead him to come to know it but also has the right to expect that the teacher has done considerable thinking about it and has come out with some definite opinions and convictions. The student wants to know what his teacher thinks. His wish to know this is not simply (as if often said when his query is pushed aside with, 'What do you think?') to know what is 'right'. It is more often his wish for both the underpinning or the stimulation of his own thinking and feeling by one who carries the authority of experienced knowledge and, thereby, the responsibility to have evolved and to transmit a perspective and point of view.

Yet another aspect of interpretation by the lecture may further and enrich the student's learning. This is the instructor's occasional presentation of his questions and doubts, his prodding pole to too readily swallowed theories, his challenge to pervasive stereotypes of thinking, his expression of difference from some 'authority' ('authority' being the person who has committed his thoughts to print!). All teachers know the phenomenon of the mind's mobilization to use of its analytic and synthesizing powers when ideas are placed in juxtaposition to one another or when that which has been taken for granted is suddenly exposed to question. Nothing is so provocative of thinking and discussion as difference. Moreover, students who are being developed to think on their own need to be given both the example and the encouragement to dare to differ, to venture out of their submission to the printed word or to the authority of great names, to pose their thinking against that of another human being. Within the brief classroom lecture the instructor may provide this encouragement; he may—or should—provide further such ideas of his own which will provoke or nourish independent thought on the student's part.

The examples that come to mind of this kind of interpretive lecture are personal ones. I offer them without undue apology because the reader is free (as was the student) to note them or let them be.

In a class discussion about the effect of the individual's past upon his present actions and feelings I noted the tendency in the students to ascribe certain inevitable results to certain childhood events recounted by the client. Something I had read of Santayana's surged to my mind. 'The past,' he said, 'cannot be re-enacted except in the language and with the contrasts imposed by the present.' I quoted this to the class and found myself delivering an impromptu on the possibility that the present may affect heavily the individual's concept and account of his past. The person who is reasonably content with his present life rarely probes his past, or when he does, his revelations are likely to be coloured by his current contentment. He will, for example, focus on gratifying experiences as well as frustrating, or he is likely to have a rationale by which to explain frustration. But the person who is unhappy sees his past through darkened lenses, and that which he sees in the forefront are the sources of his unhappiness. These are the persons whose histories are known to caseworker and psychiatrist. Perhaps some of the inevitable cause-and-effect relationships we see between past and present are not so inevitable after all?

Again, in discussion of a case of a woman who rejects her child and wishes she were back in her gratifying job again, the students brought to understanding her certain classic concepts of personality which they had taken on whole from their reading. Men with artistic flair are 'feminine'; women who want to work after marriage are 'rejecting their feminine roles'. (And this is a class full of women, many of them married, all preparing for a profession!) My question, 'What do you mean by these terms?' brought only floundering essays because 'All the authors say. . . .' I took this on in a brief lecture: their responsibility for testing the validity of what they read against their common everyday knowledge; the necessity for recognizing the culture of the second half of the twentieth century. U.S.A., as a moulder of personality as different from the culture of nineteenth-century, middle Europe; the challenge to think about what had only recently (and perhaps belatedly) struck me, which was that the tremendous majority of great artists over the ages have been men, not women. The reasons for this are not the issue; the issue is why 'artistry' is considered feminine. And so on.

In both these types of interpretive lectures there was a challenge, as can be seen, to the breakup of stereotyped thinking and of submissive learning, a sharing with the student of some difference of ideas and another point of view, a posing of questions which remain to be worked out. Typically I have found the result to be a quickening of active ideation in the student, some pleasurable relief at the permission to voice heresy, some elation at being made partner to a fresh idea, and a real revitalization of class discussion.

One further purpose, not yet named, is served by the lecture. I have let it come last because it is the purpose of expedience, and somehow that has become a tainted word. But it must be faced. Students, particularly students in a professional school, are not allowed to learn in their own time, at their own pace, in ratio to their own capacities. To the class schedule that, within each term, calls time and place of coverage and arrival, the teacher too is subject. This ought not be too readily deplored, this fact that it is required that certain learning take place within a certain time span. The very presence of these boundaries results in higher moblization of both learning and teaching energies and a more intensely meaningful relationship to the experience. So the purpose of the lecture may be to save time. There is scarcely a subject matter in the content of casework which could not be effectively dealt with by the discussion method. Since time does not permit this, the teacher must select out certain areas of content to be given to the students rather than developed by them. Obviously, the fewer of these we-are-operating-against-time lectures, the better.

The problem of numbers is another which may push the teacher to lecture against his wish and judgment. Past a certain number of students the discussion method falters. Relationship between teacher and students and among students themselves is diluted; there come to be islands of discussants in a sea of noncommunicants, or, as discussion spreads, a concomitant diffusion of focus is seen. Schools of social work, when large numbers of students are among their problems, have been among the first to give cognizance to the desirability of the discussion-size group for courses where exercise is in the use of knowledge. Suffice it to say, then, that, when for various reasons class size cannot be controlled, the teacher's responsibility increases for organizing and interpreting by way of the lecture.

The problem aspects in the use of the lecture are obvious; they are the negative phase of all that is held to be positive and educationally valuable in discussion. In the course of the lecture the mind—or at very least the musculature—of the teacher is active and engaged. The activity of the student's mind cannot be known. He may actively be taking in, he may actively be thinking of something else or he may passively be letting the flow of words wash over him and drain off.[1] Furthermore, the gaps or distortions in the student's reception cannot always be gauged, nor can the reactions and attitudes which may be roused in him and which may block or distort his reception immediately be known or dealt with. And not the least among the negatives of the lecture is the comfort it may provide for the instructor, not the comfort of feeling competent to work within a situation, but the too cosy comfort of having a situation which will work itself. ('Here it is, all written down, solid as Gibraltar, needing only my eye and voice to transmit it!') Here lies the danger that the teacher falls more in love with his formulations than with his students, and the students, sensing this, reject both him and his love object.

Happily most of these problems are not inevitable, and in the casework class, if they are understood and attended to by the teacher, need be only short lived. First, the teacher must take stock of that all-too-human inclination in himself to maintain status quo. We come to regard something which we have written down or carefully constructed in our minds as precious; besides, in the ordinary pressures of teaching life, it becomes easier to repeat earlier formulations than to develop new ones or new ways. I think particularly of the knowledge-

---

[1] 'It is difficult to find amusement during a lecture which will distract one's attention completely from the lecturer, although I have known instances in which the difficulty has been successfully overcome by patient ingenuity' Henry Sidgwick, quoted by Sir Arthur Quiller-Couch in his delightful *A Lecture on Lectures*, Harcourt, Brace and Co., New York, 1928.

giving lecture in this regard. Its term after term repetition ought, it seems to me, to signal the instructor's consideration as to whether it merits commitment to the press or the mimeograph machine so that students can read it outside class time, or whether, in the light of changes in practice, in areas of special concerns, or in the body of casework literature, it merits commitment (horrid thought!) to the wastebasket. If, however, this cut and dried lecture may be disposed of simply on its obvious faults as a teaching method, it may be seen that many of the faults commonly attributed to the lecture as a teaching method are faults not of the means *per se* but of the ways by which it is so often conveyed. The method of classroom lecture, then, warrants some consideration.

The lecture in the casework class as it has been considered here is an adjunct and supplement to teaching and learning by discussion. It sets the groundwork for class participation, or it stems from the partial formulations or not fully answered questions raised in discussion. Problems of student passivity, inattention, mistaken or distorted perceptions for which the lecture may carry blame, are dealt with largely in discussion sessions where lecture content is used, tested and perhaps reworked. As it is used in a class where discussion is the major method, it is an informal discourse, usually brief, often interspersed with student questions or comments which have been encouraged or freely allowed by the instructor.

When it is given for the purpose of providing working equipment for the student or the organizing and patterning of content already covered, it is usually prepared in advance. Even if the teacher knows the particular topic of his discourse backward and forward, as the saying goes—or perhaps one should say especially when he knows his subject matter thoroughly—preparation is incumbent upon him. This is in order that he should separate out from his store of what he knows those aspects of the material which the students need to know. What the students need to know will vary in relation to the stage of their development and the particular problem for which this new knowledge is to be used as tool. Certainly in a brief lecture to first-quarter students on the nature of a professional relationship (and hopefully this would rise out of the class's own efforts to describe and analyse it) the casework instructor would leave unsaid much of what he himself knows of relationship (its neurotic components, for example) and confine himself to developing such aspects of this phenomenon as these students at this stage of learning and experience are able to take in and use. Selection of data, then, and their logical organization in relation to the students' felt or anticipated need is a primary requisite of the advance preparation for the lecture.

The interpretive lecture, especially with the experienced teacher, may sometimes be a spontaneous delivery, generated in the sparked contact of mind to mind in discussion. This tends to be an inspired lecture. (That is, inspiration is the cause, not necessarily the effect! Yet every one of us who as student or as teacher has known the flint-and-tinder friction of mind on mind knows, too, the thrill which permeates a classroom when the bright flame of a new thought is struck up. Whether it occurs in the student or the teacher is not important for the moment. It is the birth of thought which excites both.) For this spontaneous lecture no preparation can be prescribed, I suppose, except the long steeping and reflection upon the meaning and import of a subject matter.

The interpretive lecture for which the teacher prepares, however, calls for even more than selection and logical organization. It is given, the instructor must remember, to make clear or to light up that which the student has already tackled and found obscure on unreal or confusing. Therefore the instructor must stop to analyse the nature of the problem which has been encountered by the student. Is his understanding limited by emotions for or against an idea? By the limitations of his experience? By the lack of knowledge by which to think? By the actual lack of clarity in the exposition of the theory or concepts as the student has read or heard them? It is with some idea of the particular barriers to understanding that the instructor relates himself to helping the student scale them. Fortunately, he has readily at hand certain principles of interpretation which stood him in good stead when he operated as caseworker. 'Start where the person is'—that is, start at the point of his temporary halt, though it may mean tracking back over ground already covered. Relate what is to be learned to what is already familiar to the student, because what is familiar is readily acceptable. What is familiar to him are the experiences he himself has had which, in one shape or another, are universal to all human beings. There is scarcely a feeling or an act or a theory of human emotion and behaviour which cannot be exemplified and paralleled in the life experience of the student himself or of the people he has lived with. To interpret 'identification' or 'resistance' or 'insight' or reactions to taking and giving, or feelings of loving and hating, or concepts of conscious and unconscious—to interpret these the instructor has only to play his mind imaginatively over the everyday living of the everyday student. It will yield innumerable familiar illustrations and analogies which the student can recognize without fear. That which is sufficiently familiar makes common sense, that is, it is part of the commonly accepted experience; therefore, the translation of analogy or example into common-sense principle is the next natural step for instructor and thence for student. Sometimes that which must be explained may be too threatening to the inner security of the student or may be part of what the student has repressed into unknowing. Novels, plays, biographies, even movies, abound in examples of living experience which the student may readily recognize because he can experience them vicariously and with comparative safety. Having been helped to see a tangible exemplification of an idea, he is more ready to accept the theory by which to incorporate it into his body of understood knowledge. All this requires of the instructor that in his preparation he let his mind range freely across common human experience and over the vast deep records of that experience which were writen down before formulation of their rationals was dreamed of. From these sources, which hopefully the student's humanistic education has made known to him, can be drawn the example and the precept.

The purpose of interpretation, of course, in teaching as in casework, is not simply to clarify a situation or idea for the sake of clarity or even for the sake of interest. It is for use. It aims at relating what needs newly or better to be understood to the resolution of the problem at hand. Therefore the interpretive lecture calls for the instructor's making manifest why this is being expatiated; it is not simply that 'this is something you ought to understand' but that 'this is something you ought to understand because it has usefulness to the task at which you're engaged—and this is how it relates. . . .'

Thus the lecturer who would be an interpreter of knowledge adds to the basic selection and order of his presentation of these things: his analysis of the nature of what blocks the student's understanding, his appraisal of the student's learning need at this given point, his use of homely or familiar illustrations to light up the unknown and relate it to the known, his translation of example into its general significance, and his making clear the usefulness of this part to the student's understanding and work.

And now with the purpose of his lecture clearly before him and its content selected to meet that purpose, the teacher is ready to communicate what he has to say to his listeners.

Now arise the dicta of the public speaking class to plague him: do not read, talk to the people; speak the speech trippingly, I pray you; eyes front, neither on the floor nor ceiling fix them; and so on. So many of these adjurations are useless to the teacher. By age and by experience he is already patterned as a person and therefore as a platform personality. He cannot cultivate an engaging presence or quick wit or warmth at will, nor can he feel self-assured with the imitation of another's techniques. All of us have known the teacher who by his brilliance and charm lighted up new worlds for us; and we have known him who by his wit and legerdemain wove such a spell as left us empty when he was done. All of us have known, too, the teacher who, taking shelter behind his subject matter, set it as a wall between him and his students; and we have known him, too, who, for all that he had neither delivery nor personality, so loved his subject and the students who came to it that what he said was not readily forgotten. So, then, what are the attributes of 'good' lecture method?

They are not essentially different from those of any good communication. The desire, the impelling wish, to relate one's self to another by speech comes first. In teaching, this desire takes on the added motivation of helpfulness—'I want to help you to know what you will find good'—and the fact that the student has chosen to be here bespeaks his partnership, though temporarily it may be a silent one. To communicate begins with a recognition of the one by the other. On the teacher's part it begins by his thinking about these particular students with whom he is to share his subject. The recognition of them is made manifest when, as he faces the class, he looks, not at a blur of faces, but at the individual persons with whom he is talking. 'With whom he is talking' is perhaps the key phrase. One may talk 'to' and one may talk 'at'; both of these imply disregard or even obliteration of the reactions of the other. To talk 'with' is to maintain the sense of intercommunication, even though one side of the communication is silent. That side makes itself known to him who talks 'with' by the lighted face of understanding, the frown of disagreement, the narrowed eye of scepticism, the blankness of boredom. (True, all of us have known certain students who have developed the fine art of fixing the instructor with a bright eye while the mind goes freely woolgathering, but generally the eye and the attention are caught together). Related as he is to the persons with whom he talks, the lecturer notes their responses. As a former caseworker he has long been an observer and interpreter of human behaviour, and part of his professional skill has lain in his ability to cut and shape content and direction to the needs which behaviour expresses. These abilities are in considerable part transferable into the classroom. The lecturer who is in contact with his hearers can give them indication that he is aware

H

of their responsive behaviour and takes it into account. If conditions permit, he can cut or expand and shape his subject to the needs which are being made manifest. At the very least he can give recognition to the responses: 'I can see that most of you recognize what I'm talking about as a common problem. Let's explore it further.' Or 'I see that several of you disagree with me. Let me finish just this, and then I'll give you your innings.' In the student this recognition by the lecturer rouses a sense of relatedness; he is more likely to feel at one with the person who talks with him, whose obvious interest is not to cram him with subject matter but to invite him by eye and manner to partake of it.

Good communication in the classroom is for the purpose of transacting business. Perhaps it is presumptuous to set down a fact so obvious. Yet, to hark back to casework practice again, it is not only the inexperienced practitioner who needs to be reminded on occasion that a good relationship with a client is not an end in itself but is one of the elements which makes the casework possible. So in the classroom, the establishment of relationship between lecturer and class is for the business of transmitting a content of knowledge and ideas which is held to be of value. When this is fully accepted by the teacher and when he has conviction as to the worth of his subject matter, the self-consciousness which sometimes besets him or his anxiousness as to whether or not he will get over may noticeably subside. It is not he who must get over. It is his subject matter. As he keeps his focus squarely on that in its intimate relationship to his object matter, his students, his lecture will carry itself—that is, his method will flow out of content-in-a-relationship. Of course, the personal talents and attributes of individual teachers will make one a brilliant and another a prosaic lecturer, one an artist and another an artisan in communication. But the basic essentials for good teaching hold for all: that the teacher know his subject matter thoroughly and feelingly and that he relate to the learner with pleasure and respect. To these essentials the teacher must add his thought and clarity as to what specific purpose in furthering the students' learning his communication is to serve. When these elements combine, there is little relation between the lecture and exciting oratory or deadening pedantry. It may be seen for what, at best, it is: a means by which knowledge may be imparted, organized and interpreted for its immediate use by the participating student.

8

TEACHING CASEWORK BY THE DISCUSSION METHOD*

HELEN HARRIS PERLMAN

In these days of the frantic effort to communicate with one's fellow-men before it is too late, the discussion method is used as widely and sometimes as indiscriminately as vitamin pills. From solving problems of world maladjustment to personal maladjustment, from deciding 'Shall we have an H-bomb?' to 'Shall we invite boys to our party?' from promoting good legislation to promoting good fellowship, from fostering good leadership to fostering good learning, the discussion method is held to be a means.[1] It is readily understandable that, with a means so widely used for so many diverse purposes, there has come to be some rather loose thinking about and loose applications of this method of problem-solving.

Gather a group of teachers of casework together about the subject of classroom discussion, and there will be general and warm agreement that discussion is a good teaching method and a good learning means. But one of the surest ways to bring conversation about 'discussion' to a dead stop is to ask, 'What is a discussion?' The origin of 'to discuss' means 'to shake apart'. In order to 'shake apart' both the silence and the question, this attempt at descriptive definition is offered.

Discussion is thinking out loud together with others. Or, to put it more formally, a discussion is a reasoned verbal communication between two or more persons. (Emotions may be involved or may underlie the reasoning, but the conscious effort is to hold emotion in the check of intellectual processes. If emotion breaks loose, rational communication breaks down). A discussion proceeds from a point of mutual clarity and agreement as to its focal issues or facts or assumptions, and these constitute the framework of reference and gauge of relevance. There

* Published in *The Social Service Review*, Vol. XXIV, No. 3, September, 1950.

[1] Not long ago I observed a classroom discussion by six-year-olds. The issue was whether Ralph should have told Dick to 'sock up' on James and bloody his nose. Why should one person tell another person to do *his* dirty work for him? And besides, even if he did, why should Dick be foolish enough to do what some other kid tells him to? Especially if it's wrong? I was pleasantly aware that a generation ago in the first grade, Ralph and Dick, not the question, would have been shaken apart, and boys and question, all, would have been consigned to the dark silence of the cloakroom.

must be, further, mutual agreement that the significance of these facts, issues or assumptions is open to question or interpretation or differing judgment. Discussion begins with a question of opinion, of differing interpretation of accepted premises or facts. The activity in a discussion is the exercise of minds in an effort to 'shake apart'—to explore, analyse, evaluate and come to some conclusion or judgment of a situation, idea or act. The conclusion come to may be that a conclusion cannot be arrived at, that the issue remains one of preference, opinion, personal value—but this will have been established by communicated thought rather than by impulsive espousal. All discussions have these elements in common.

The classroom discussion, however, poses some special considerations. It is a method used towards a specified end: that within a given period of time students will have incorporated a certain content of knowledge, certain habits of thought, and certain ways of operation. Within a university, as in any formal school system, a sequence of courses leads to a teminal point at which it is certified that the student has mastered certain experiences and has arrived at a certain point in his development. Within any one course a certain section of knowledge and certain exercise in the use of that knowledge must be experienced and learned within a limited period of time. Classroom discussion is, then, a bounded discussion. It is bounded by what is to be learned within what period of time.

It may be argued that discussion which is 'freewheeling' and which comes to have content and take shape via the group's own recognition and self-disciplined efforts is in the long run the richest and truest learning experience. This may be true. It may be argued that discussion wherein members of the group are free to say that which they are moved to say is 'democratic'. This may or may not be true, depending upon some definition of 'democratic' and its differentiation from 'anarchy' or 'laissez faire'. It may be argued that discussion, better than other teaching methods, can be paced to the students' learning rate, which does not necessarily conform to the quarter or semester system. Both these statements are true, provided 'should' is not slipped in for 'can'. But the reality of the ends to be achieved within the limits of given time is implacable. No one knows better than the teacher how brief is the life of a course and how fleeting time. Today the neophyte gives hail; tomorrow the graduate says farewell; and in the span of a few deep breaths the teacher and the former student are on the same platform (each with some mixed feelings), each performing as a discussant of a professional paper.

If it is accepted that classroom discussion must be a discussion controlled by considerations of what is to be learned within what period of time, then the role of the teacher in classroom discussion begins to come clear. He cannot beguile himself into thinking he is just a 'catalytic agent'. Nor is he a 'group leader' in the general sense of nurturing, over an unspecified time, a group's capacity to achieve its self-determined ends. He is a 'leader' in the explicit sense of having the authority and obligation to guide and to direct and often to require. He is an 'instructor' in that at given time and place he must inject some knowledge by means of which the class can go forward. He must take responsibility both for stimulating discussion and for controlling it, both for releasing the students' energies and for insistently directing them to the task for which they have been freed. He is responsible not only to promote movement but, literally, to 'steer the course' so that direction is not lost. He must not only keep the class going but help it arrive.

It cannot, then, be happily assumed that in classroom teaching discussion is good for the soul. Whether or not it is a good means of teaching and learning depends upon the teacher's clear understanding of what it is, what its relation is to the specified educational goals,[1] and finally upon the teacher's working out such ways and means as will promote and manage the fulsome use of discussion in achieving these goals. What follows here is limited to considerations of the use of discussion as a method of teaching. Its specific content is that of the use of this method in the teaching of social casework in a school of social work, but perhaps, in parts, it may have some wider applications.

To observe a good discussion is to be impressed with its apparent spontaneity, freedom, the combustion of ideas among the participants, and by the keen skill of the leader in provoking new thought and drawing its varied strands together. One tends to think of this teacher or discussion leader as a 'natural', as one who, without preparation is ready to take on what comes. Perhaps he is. Or perhaps his readiness is the product of preparation. And perhaps some skills have become second nature to him which were once carefully learned and incorporated by prepared practice.

Many of these skills are those which the casework teacher learned and practised in the one-to-one discussions of the casework process itself. Transferred with necessary modifications to the class group,

---

[1] The educational purpose of discussion as a means of learning by doing (learning to think, to communicate, to co-operate, etc.) is not included in this article largely because of space considerations.

they will remain familiar to him. One of these skills is attentive listening, not just to the words being said but to the import of what is being said. Following on this (and in the experienced discussion leader it is virtually spontaneous with it) is the effort to make connection between that which has been said and that which preceded it or that which might logically follow it. This sequence or interplay of statements and questions the discussion leader must relate to the major questions or issues in discussion. The ability to do this is the ability to maintain focus upon a nuclear idea at the same time as its radiations are followed and then drawn back to the central body. (This, too, is a skill well known to the caseworker. The client's story may lead into labyrinthine paths, where both he and the caseworker will be lost except as the caseworker has learned to maintain a central focus and to help the client relate himself and his involved discussion back to that). The discussion leader, then, must be able to focus discussion so that, for all its diversity, it maintains an essential wholeness, a basic unity. The awareness of basic unity needs, of course, to be shared with the discussion participants who, in their involvement with one or another idea, may have lost the direction. Periodically, then, the discussion leader pulls together related parts of the discussion; if discussion is visualized as the spokes of a wheel radiating from the hub, the leader may be said to 'rim the wheel'.

Within its unity a good discussion must have movement. It must progress. For all that it may eddy about a question or idea at any given moment or at other times leap across logical barriers, it must move forward in a progression of clarification to the resolution which is being sought. The leader of a good discussion must be able, then, to help the group keep aware of where it is going, whether it is getting there, and when it has arrived. This means that the leader himself must have a good sense of direction and a clear perception both of immediate and of more remote goals. And when, as sometimes happens, the release of tension through self-expression leaves the discussants feeling content, the leader must goad them one step further—'So what? Where does that get us? To what conclusion do you come?' (Thus, too, though in different manner, does the caseworker help his client take the step of coming to grips with the implications for his action of that which he has come to understand).

That a discussion should have unity, direction and movement can reasonably be assured through the instructor-leader's advance preparation; and, if he is not a 'natural', he may come to act and feel like one. Discussion in casework classes most frequently arises out of consideration of the specific case material at hand which has been studied in the light of certain reading or foreknowledge, from these materials general understanding and principles of the life-process and the helping process are sought. Each class period partializes the whole of the progressive sequence of cases and their teaching content. Each class period requires of the instructor, then, that he structure its major teaching points, related to the structure and content of the course in its entirety. The casework teacher, whatever method he will use, comes to his class not with a case which, by virtue of its drama and interest, is bound to evoke many reactions from many students. He comes rather with a case whose teaching values and principles he has been able to extract, formulate and relate both to that which the student already knows and to that which he is to come to know. He has set down his major teaching points. These are the points around which the student's learning is to spin itself.

If discussion is to be the means toward that learning, then the questions which will provoke thinking in the desired direction can be formulated in advance. Immediately as this is done, possible student responses and reactions suggest themselves. In the quiet and safety of his own office the discussion leader may have that fantasy rehearsal which prepares him to expect even the unexpected and to be able to deal with it. Perhaps it is needless to say that this is no rehearsal of the posture and the technique. It is the anticipation of the possible ideas which may be or need to be evoked by the central questions. It enables the leader to plan how stalemate might be avoided, how speculation can be encouraged or curbed, how movement may be propelled from generalization to the specific or the other way about, and so on. Finally, the discussion leader may prepare by setting down some rough formulation of the possible conclusions to which the class may come. By this means he has his goals in mind, and at the moment of summation he is not desperately dependent upon memory to serve him in rimming the wheel.

One danger may be inherent in such careful planning—the danger of overplanning and subsequent rigidity. Driving for the answer in the teacher's mind, insistence that the class move from Roman I to Arabic I in the teacher's outline, although all the class push and excitement is focused on what is Roman II, Arabic 3, in the lesson plan—this is rigidity which may lay the cold hand of death on a discussion. Let the students discuss Roman II, Arabic 3. They are impelled to do so, and impelling energies must be captured and harnessed for learning. If the logic is inevitable that Roman II must follow Roman I, this will make itself manifest as discussion boils, or the instructor may point it up: 'But you'll notice that we haven't established the evidence on which to decide this', or 'You're assuming that thus and so is the case. Are we agreed on that?' Life as the student lives it and as the caseworker will find it does not occur in outline form. Perhaps the most persuasive instruction in the need for logical thinking is the students' experience of becoming enmeshed in a melee of reactions and impulsive ideas and a demonstration by the instructor of how logical process may serve to extricate them.

The teacher who teaches by discussion without a working outline runs many risks. Unless he is an old hand at the method, his own sense of comfort, that equilibrium in him which is essential to his being able to listen to others, follow and remember their arguments, will not be steady. Even the outline which after being set down is never used is reassuring, like a portlight in a storm. Without an outline it will be difficult for the teacher to maintain clarity as to where the discussion should be going and when it has arrived. Along with his students he may be swept away by colourful or dramatic details which are interesting but irrelevant. Or he may find that he and the class have followed a tangent and that they are about to fall off into nothingness. Or the unexpected ring of the hour bell signals the end, and the students and their thoughts are left loose and ravelled. Bells may call the close to even the best of discussions, of course, but the prepared instructor is able, by virtue of his preparation, to take hold of even that last moment to say 'Here is where we are; there is where we have yet to go; that is where we will begin next time.'

The probability is that the teacher inexperienced in the use of prepared discussion may be enslaved by his outline; but, as he gains comfort with experience he becomes master of what he now knows to be a tool.

There remains one further and important value in the instructor's advance preparation of discussion. He can help the student to come prepared. At the first class meeting some learning task is set for the student, because as early as possible he must begin to be active in his learning. He may be sent to some reading of theory; he may be assigned a case for reading 'and discussion'; he may be told that today's discussion will be continued. Whatever it is, he will prepare for class with more thoughtfulness and selectivity if the major problems for consideration are posed for him by the instructor. The book will be read not in order to store away a batch of knowledge but instead it will be put to immediate use to illuminate the problems that have been set before him. The case will be read, not alone for its highlights of human interest, but in the search for such understanding as will clarify the problems posed. Even the prospect of continuing discussion will be anticipated and mentally prepared for within the perspective and focus of formulated questions. Outside the class, then, the questions or problems posed by the teacher provide stimulus and focus for learning. To the ensuing class the student comes ready to participate and share in discussion, for he is already chewing on the food for thought which the teacher has set before him.

So much for what goes on behind the scenes on instructor's and student's part in preparing for discussion. Its acting-out takes place in the classroom. Communication begins. It begins with the eyes. The leader of which is to be good discussion must begin by looking at the discussants, must say to each with his eyes, 'I see you, I recognize you, I am content (and often glad!) to be with you.'

Not much time should pass before the instructor should have identified his individual students and should be able to address them by name. Everyone of us knows the gratification of being recognized and named in a group and, conversely, the annoyance at being considered anonymous. But beyond the good human relations involved is the consideration of what effect such recognition has upon participation in the work of a class. To be simply a nameless person in a classroom offers an easy 'out' from responsibility; to be specifically known to fellow-students and teacher is to be impelled to live up to the concept of ourselves with which we invest our names. In the small group this presents no problem. In the large class the instructor who is to know his students must develop devices by which to do it. The use of a seating chart for a few sessions so that a student stays 'put' long enough to be identified (and students are pleased to conform to this when they know its purpose); the calling of roll, not for an attendance check but with attentive taking in of the distinctive features of the respondent; the check of class names against photographs which often are part of admission materials—these are among the means by which 'the student' may quickly become 'this particular student' to the instructor, and anonymity may give way to responsible identity.

For those reasons which make it necessary that classroom discussion be bounded and focused, all its participants ought to be apprised of the purpose and the rules of the game. These do not need repetition from class to class once the pattern of classroom learning behaviour is established, but at the students' beginning in a course sequence it is well to share them openly. Details and exceptions are best left out, they will not be remembered because the students are too busy dealing with their feelings about whether they do or do not like the person, clothes, voice, etc., of the instructor. But some simple general statement of how we will function together and what will be expected of the student in in the way of classroom participation (along with other general requirements) and to what purpose we operate as we do helps to ready the student for his responsibility and his role.

From the beginning, the tone which the leader should set is one of comfortableness with the subject matter and with the students so that, in response, the student will feel comfortable with subject matter, teacher and his fellow-students. This comfort is in no wise equivalent to relaxation or pleasant inertia. It is rather the poised equilibrium and readiness for action which comes about when no attack from the outside is anticipated and when attack from within the person himself (such as his feelings of inadequacy or hostility or anxiousness) are minimal or absent. Within the relationship between himself and the class the discussion leader can do much to create an atmosphere of personal safety and to help in some small degree even that student whose inner malaise may be personal rather than situational.

The individual caseworker has long operated by the adage, 'Accept the individual but not necessarily his act'. This is readily applied in the classroom situation. Each student is listened to with equal attentiveness and respect. His right to difference from the leader or others in the group is given full recognition. Except as it is manifestly not true (as with the student who momentarily feels mischievous or negative), the motivation behind what the student says is assumed to be his honest wish to clarify his own thought or to contribute to group thinking. There is no place here for a show of the annoyance or impatience or downright despair which the leader may sometimes feel in response to a student's comments. Nor is there place for the caustic or witty thrust at what seems ludicrous or absurd. The leader would be less than human if he did not feel these and other emotions in response to what he hears. But, like the disciplined caseworker, he subjects his feelings to vigilant control. His business is to help others to feel sufficiently safe and accepted that they dare to move forward.

The probability, however, is that the teacher of casework tends to err less in the direction of attack on the student and more in the direction of over-protection, of accepting the student, his act, and his communication too wholly and too uncritically. Trained as he has been in the tradition of handling people with care, dealing with them so that hurt is not knowingly inflicted, giving them personal support while they struggle to work on their problems, the caseworker-turned-teacher is likely to come to the classroom trailing clouds of 'treatment' in his wake. He is likely to sidestep correction of an erroneous idea or challenge of an illogical opinion for fear that he may hurt feelings or undermine the student's self-confidence or interfere with his normal rate of growth. And the result may be the discussion where everyone, or nearly everyone, has expressed himself, everything or nearly everything has been accepted as 'right', and there is a temporary glow that 'we are as one'. Until the student leaves the classroom. Then he, who proposed that $a + b = c$ and he who suggested that $a + b = x$ begin to argue as to which was right and they are left to their own confusions.

The teacher's clarity as to the difference between the discussion as a therapeutic experience and as an educational experience rests upon clarity as to the purpose and content of a school course and the function of the teacher in bringing that purpose and content to life. But, even where this is not fully grasped, an understanding of the nature of growth and learning leads to the recognition that while the student must be accepted, those fragments or parts of his thinking which he produces need not be. The fact is that all human growth is stimulated by *acceptance and expectation*. *Acceptance* provides the benign climate within which safety and nurture are experienced; *expectation* provides the stimulus and challenge to reach out, strive, struggle, 'come one step out of safety'. Implicit in casework (and perhaps progress would be hastened if this were more often made explicit) are certain expectations by the caseworker of the client; acceptance is the support and nurture towards this end. Within the educational situation expectation is open and explicit. Consistently, certain tasks are set for the student to master, and they are progressively demanding. The student's ability to perform them is matched against standards and within time limits. The teacher must expect, then, as well as accept, and in courses which prepare the student for professional excellence the expectation is that he will learn to think straight, to see inconsistencies, to use words accurately, etc. Therefore, while the student is sustained by acceptance, his utterances must be dealt with so that discussion will not be simply an experience in self-expression but an experience in self-reaching for further learning.

There are a number of ways by which the instructor's attitudes and management can support the integrity of the individual student at the same time as the irrelevant or rambling or erroneous contribution is directly dealt with. The warmth of good humour provides an equable climate for comfort. Good humour is tolerant and understanding, and the laughter that occurs within it is laughter *with*, never laughter *at*, the person. The depersonalization of that which might be interpreted as attack is helpful toward maintaining the student's self-respect: 'I'm sorry to have to cut you off, Miss Black, but time's the villain of the piece, you know'. Universalization of fault (when this is valid) helps the student who has produced it to feel that he is not different, that his error is a common one: 'All of us are prone to vague generalizations when we've not thought something through. Mr White has said what a lot of us were probably thinking'. Or, 'This is a natural and understandable mistake you're making, Miss Brown. I'm glad you brought it out so that all of us can work on it'. Maintaining the student's sense of his group membership, that he is always part of group effort is reassuring: 'I'm afraid we're going off the track, Mr Green—it's a temptation for all of us. But let's hold ourselves to the point'. And, of course, the accrediting and support of that which can validly be used to promote problem-solving serves always to buoy up the student's self-esteem: 'I'd seriously question the conclusion you've come to, Miss Pink, but some of the points you've made along the way are awfully good. Let's look at them.'

An important means in all learning is by imitation and identification. Student attitudes, not only towards that which they are learning but towards those with whom they work together, are subtly but surely shaped by the attitudes of the instructor-leader. Vital to the students' professional performance will be an ability to hear others out with attentiveness, to control their negative feelings against a speaker, and to deal with what is being said rather than with the sayer. This grace of human relations and this foundation for clarity of thinking comes in some part to be consciously and unconsciously incorporated by class members as it is seen and steadfastly maintained by their leader.

Even with the best of discussion management, however, problems are likely to be encountered, troubling to the instructor and sometimes to the class group. Every teacher knows those extremes of the active-passive class curve. The consistently quiet student is often troubling because he creates dead spots in discussion, difficult because impassive silence defies interpretation—(is he with us? beyond? behind?)—and because he is not carrying his share of responsibility. The over-active discussant, on the other hand, takes more than his share of time and attention, may race ahead of the class, or bog it down in his own personal mire, or put other students to flight. Within these two problem spots in class discussion are differences which call for different handling by the instructor. The aggresive discussant may be one of two distinct types. One is an active, eager, searching learner, thirsty for knowledge and impulsively running towards it. His feeling is that learning is good, he wants to partake of it freely, and sometimes his greed overcomes his awareness that others may also want to share. Because this person is with the instructor (wants to be with him too much), because he feels positive toward his learning experience, it is only his behaviour and not he himself that needs dealing with. Within the discussion situation this can be dealt with, firmly and good-humouredly, by his being asked to hold on to himself, to give others a chance, or even by passing over his insistent hand with a friendly glance of acknowledgement, etc. He is likely to understand and accept limitations on himself.

The other type among the over-active discussants is the student whose approach to learning is by mobilization for fight, whose feelings of suspicion, potential danger and negativism are roused by the new or the different. He must attack or spar with each new idea or the purveyor of such ideas. As a person whose first feeling is *against* (though he may come eventually to be passionately *for*), he is often unloved by class and teacher. But he may serve a very useful purpose. The gadfly and the doubting Thomas are antidotes against the smugness or slickness which may develop in a class or in an instructor. The probing quality of a hostile mind may take a good poke at frozen formulations. Furthermore, this one individual's expression of negativism or doubt may be the echo of what was in the minds of many in the class who lacked the courage to say so. When this is so, it can be seen in the brightened eyes of the other students or in the readiness with which they'll move into the fray. If, on the other hand, this is a one-person problem, this too can be known to the observant instructor by the manifestations of the elaborate patience or the cooling interest which appears in the class. The problem of repeatedly expressed negativism or fixed ideas can be dealt with in only a limited way in the classroom. Again, the rules of discussion are invoked rather than the pardonable ire of the instructor-leader. 'Is anyone else concerned with this issue? If not, let's not take class time for it.' Or, 'I'm going to interrupt you right here, Mr X, because we can't thrash that out here. I'll be glad to discuss it with you after class though'. The more troubling problem is whether this student will ever be able to arrive at feeling at one with the subject matter he is to master and the persons with whom he is to operate professionally. This question will have to be faced with the student in individual conference, and his ability to change his classroom behaviour will be partial test of his ability to become a professional person.

Among the silent ones, too, two different types are to be found. The one is the submissive learner, students who have been drubbed into passivity by their previous learning experience, whether at home or in school. They take what is fed them obediently, uncritically, and if they are resistive, they are not conscious of it. They taste without particular pleasure, often swallow whole, and tend to be resigned to some of the miseries of indigestion. They are troubling to the instructor, not simply because they may be a passive load to be carried by the rest of the class, but, more, because of the question they pose as to their eventual ability to give nourishment to their profession.

The second major group of students who do not readily participate in discussion are those who are active but introspective learners. Their mental activity during discussion is readily seen in the responsiveness of eye, in the lights and shadows which play across their faces, in the quality of alertness in their very posture. Sometimes, as only written assignments will reveal, the most deeply thoughtful, critical, insightful students are to be found among those silent participants. Here the problem is less that they do not make themselves vocal but more that they work as lone operators rather than in co-operative venture. However, the classroom is not the most vital testing ground of their ability to co-operate in relationship with others. For these students as well as for all others, active field work practice, client-worker, worker-co-worker, worker-supervisor relationships pose the test of ability to give of one's self and take in of another.

But so long as the use of the discussion method in the classroom aims at the development, through practice, of certain behaviour, it is incumbent upon the instructor-leader to attempt to engage the non-discussants, be they the silent-passive or the silent-active ones, in open participation. There are several ways by which this can be done. While a course which is to use the discussion method starts with the instructor's sharing with the students the ways by which they will operate and the wherefores of such ways, it may be necessary to repeat something of this as the course goes along—'You'll remember we talked in our beginning session about the values for our professional development in sharing our thinking, in working together at difficult problems. Right now about three people seem to be carrying the lug.' Sometimes the silent student can be called on. This should happen not when he is likely to be caught unprepared or unrelated but rather when the opportunity for response offers him easy range (as 'What is your reaction to . . . ?') or when his face makes plain that he is at one with the ongoing discussion. Sometimes the instructor may respond to the communication from the student which comes via the written paper by adding to his comments the suggestion or the wish that the student share his good thinking or his interesting ideas with the rest of the class. And sometimes, again, the problem needs to be dealt with between instructor and student in individual conference with the instructor's attempt to understand the meaning of the student's nonparticipation and to help the student understand the value to his own growth of risking himself.

But the teacher using the discussion method must not be seduced by the happy active noises of discussion and the spread of participation into believing that this in itself is an educational experience. Communication is not enough. Planned education requires that the student learn by doing certain things in certain ways. Classroom discussion has as its major purpose the establishment and the exercise of given ways by which professional communication may be assured. These ways are based on habits of sound thinking, and the teacher leading discussion must hold himself and his students to the exercise of these habits.

Thinking begins with an observed or perceived fact or situation or condition. Whether data will be observed or perceived accurately or not depends in large part on whether mental vision is clear. Its most frequent dimming or distortion is due to emotions or attitudes which come between the observer and that which is perceived. Spontaneously with perception comes ideation—that which is seen is 'read into', that is, inferences are drawn from the theoretical or experiential knowledge of the observer and are attached to the data. From among these speculations some selection is made and a supposition or hypothesis is formed which invests the data with meaning. This formulation, like perception, may be coloured and shaped by attitudes, feelings, convictions and prejudice. Now the validity of this explanation of meaning is taken apart and tested by such facts or knowledge as may be brought to bear on it. In this process of analysis, account is taken of which is known, what is inferred, what is supposed, what can or cannot be validated, what remains to be known and what can be put together into a synthesis called judgment or conclusion.

Obviously, every problem we encounter in our personal or professional lives does not demand for its solution the whole of this thinking process. Even when it does, we are often not conscious of having taken these steps because of the spontaneity and speed with which they may be leaped. But teaching and learning from the materials and processes of casework makes particularly necessary the carefulness and the disciplined habits of mind which assure good thinking. Casework, concerned as it is with understanding and helping live human beings in live social situations, tends to rouse in the student considerable subjective involvement, impulsive assumption, prejudice for or against, emotionalized thinking. These reactions will distort or blur the clarity of his perceptions and his judgment unless he has become habituated by practice to the discipline of thoughtfulness. What the student thinks and how he thinks can best be known and best be dealt with as he communicates and shares his thinking aloud in class discussion. To differentiate fact from inference, to separate what is known from what is felt, and what is felt from what is thought, to widen and deepen the range of ideas, to develop and test meanings by pooled knowledge and experience, to scrutinize interpretations in the light of knowledge, to weigh pros and cons, to arrive at considered judgments—for all these purposes the discussion provides opportunity and offers experience and practice in the communication, sharing, testing and synthesis of thinking.

Discussion provides this opportunity. Whether it will be used depends of course directly upon the teacher. To his assumed ability to think around a point and then *to* it he must, as a discussion leader, bring a store of ready energy and patient persistence in order to spur on and yet hold his students to the rigorous demands of sound thinking and clear communication.

Here is an illustration, first, of what may pass for discussion, and, then, of what 'good' discussion would require.

Overheard in a first-term casework class:[1]

Instructor: We'll begin today with our study of the Borden case. What kind of person would you say Mr Borden is?

Miss Black: I feel he's a person with deep dependency needs— somewhat pauperized.

Mr White: I don't get that at all. It seems to me he's a victim of economic circumstance. If his factory shuts down, what can he do but apply for relief?

Miss Green: That's true. He's a victim of circumstance. But, just the same, the way he talks about not wanting relief shows he's afraid of becoming dependent.

Mr White: Nobody likes to take relief.

Miss Blue: I don't know what Miss Green means—'the way he talks about not wanting relief'.

[1] This is a synthetic, not a verbatim, report.

Miss Green: I mean he talks about it in an immature and dependent sort of way.

Mr Gray: I think we ought to define our terms. What do we mean by 'mature' and 'dependent'?
Silence.

Miss Pink: I feel the caseworker did a very nice job when she explained to Mr Borden his right to relief. It made him feel better.

Mr White: Is that what a caseworker is for? I mean, should a caseworker try to help people resign themselves to their fate?

Miss Pink: No-o-but—
Silence, while Miss Pink struggles with this problem.

Instructor: Mr Brown, what do you think?

This purports to be a discussion. The participation is widespread, but students are not communicating with one another. They are simply expressing themselves. Several are struggling to achieve a common base of understanding, but their efforts are not supported. In this short span of talk several different problems have been thrown into the ring, but no one of them has been focused for scrutiny. The instructor by his silence implies that anything goes or that everything goes well.

An interpolated 'playback' of this class activity may illustrate how the instructor might have made it a good discussion:

The instructor begins by asking, 'What kind of person would you say Mr Borden is?' Mr Borden's fate will not be determined in this class. What kind of person he actually is, or was, may never be known to us. What the instructor's question seeks to bring out is this: From your observations of Mr B. as he is described, as he talks and acts in this account, to what conclusions do you come as to the meaning of his characteristics and behaviour? It follows that evidence would have to support conclusion or that the latter would be tested against the former, that meanings ascribed to the facts would have to be supported by accepted or understood theory or knowledge, that implications would need to be made explicit, and so on. In short, what the instructor is asking for is an exercise of the student's use of his knowledge, observations and reasoning processes as a means by which a person or a problem may be understood.

Miss Black 'feels' that he has 'deep dependency needs' and that he is 'somewhat pauperized'. Perhaps she has the gift of intuition. Whether it is preconscious thinking or is some as yet unexplained psychic

I

phenomenon is less important than that intuition cannot be taught and cannot be dealt with in a classroom. Miss Black must be held to share the basis for her 'feeling'. What is her evidence? Or what are the reasons by which she arrives at this conclusion? And what do the terms she uses mean? They are often vague, sometimes emotionalized. Do we all mean the same thing when we say 'dependency'?

Mr White seems to be reacting as much to Miss Black as to the client. His flat substitute opinion is as suspect as Miss Black's. He, too, needs to be held to breaking up a sweeping generality and examining it in the light of evidence and to recognizing that being a 'victim of economic circumstances' hardly rules out 'dependency' as a personality trait.

Miss Green steps in, trying to accept both judgments, and she proffers substantiation of one, but this is not drawn out. Again, here, the instructor might have pointed up that some evidence was being offered and have followed through on it—'How do you mean "the way he talks"—what do you infer here?'

Since this is allowed to stand, Mr White makes another generalization to support his interpretation of the client. 'Is that true? How do you know that, Mr White?'—by this challenge the instructor discourages the use of the flat dogmatic statement which throws analysis to the winds and makes other discussants feel either helpless or contentious.

Miss Blue disregards Mr White and asks Miss Green for evidence, and Miss Green goes in a circle. She needs help to go back a step or two and to say exactly what she observes in Mr Borden which leads her to impute meanings she gives. Mr Gray attempts to cut the circle by pressing for a definition.—'That's good. Let's be clear that we understand our terms.'

But silence follows, because definition is hard work and risky business besides, since it may reveal the gaps in your thinking. Now the instructor must move in to support the effort being made in the right direction and to clarify and focus what has now become a dual problem—that posed by the question itself and that posed by the direction the discussion has taken. He may readily recognize with the group their understandable reluctance to work at a problem rather than to 'feel' about it. He must restate the question and point out how it needs to be approached, may suggest clarification of terms, etc. No one student needs to be held culpable; it is the idea and the method of thought which are being attacked by the instructor.

But since this has not happened, Miss Pink steps in. Miss Pink wants a peaceful settlement, or she hasn't been paying attention. She changes the subject, appraising the worker's treatment. Without attacking Miss Pink's motivation or failure to connect, the instructor must show her that her contribution is irrelevant at present—'That's an aspect of the case we'll be coming to later, Miss Pink. Hold it, will you, so we won't go off the track?'

Instead, Mr White leaps to challenge Miss Pink's point. (Mr White is in there fighting something or somebody again! He'll need some thought). He poses a problem of professional ideology. It floors Miss Pink and her fellow-students because it is the unexpected introduction of a new consideration and a different type of problem and also, perhaps, because at this stage in the students' learning it is a troubling question which they have tended to repress rather than resolve. This calls not for the expression of another discussant's opinion but for the teacher's authority, as leader, to do several things: He must step in to make clear that this is an important question which Mr White has raised and that it introduces a problem different from what was being worked on. By the rules of good discussion it may be discussed in its general aspects with the group's recognition that, for the nonce, the problem of diagnosis of Mr Borden is being tabled. When some conclusion has been reached by the class as to whether or not 'casework is to resign people to their fate', the help given Mr Borden can be viewed against the concepts agreed upon. Or it is possible to table the question until treatment of Mr Borden is discussed when it may be reintroduced —and so on.

It goes without saying, of course, that had Miss Black's first response been dealt with as suggested, the discussion would never have evolved as it did, because the teacher's management of it would have shaped and changed its nature. That management would, as illustrated above, have resulted in the rejection of loose statements and terms, of emotionalized thinking, of irrelevancies and would have substituted the requirement of common understanding or agreement on terms and issues, the maintenance of focus, the use of knowledge and reasoning processes as the means to judgments, and the frank recognition of speculation, inference, or absence of knowledge, when they occur. In short, had those means of thinking aloud together been required, the students would have experienced the healthy rigours of good discussion.

To rim this many-spoked wheel. The educational value of discussion is the exercise of the student's mind in habits of clear thinking and clear communication. Within a given course of study the use of the discussion method is affected not alone by this purpose but also by considerations of content to be learned within a given time unit. By virtue of these several factors and of his necessary perspectives as to direction and goals of study, the teacher must be both prepared and active in his role as instructor-leader. His preparation consists of seeing and using each class session as a forward-moving unit of the whole course structure and of formulating and sharing the essential questions to be 'shaken apart' toward their resolution. His activity consists of conveying to his students his understanding acceptance of their feelings and foibles and, at the same time, his understandable expectation that their interest and efforts will be brought to working on problems of common concern. Within this tempered climate which the teacher sets, he must repeatedly and continuously encourage the students' exercise in those habits of shaking-apart, evaluating, reorganizing and sharing their thinking. By these means discussions which begin as verbalized reaction may develop into intelligible and responsible communications of knowledge and ideas.

9

THE PLACE OF HELP IN SUPERVISION*

CHARLOTTE TOWLE

SUPERVISION in social agencies has been defined as an administrative process in the conduct of which staff development is a major concern. Supervision is a process in the conduct of which the supervisor has three functions—administration, teaching and helping. His mid-position has significance in the performance of each of these functions, and notably in helping.[1]

The supervisor in the full-fledged performance of his functions as administrator and teacher helps the student learn. Why specify the helping function separately rather than leaving it as implicit in the other two? Some educators do not specify it separately. I have done so because I think we should be aware of activity which is not implicit in all teaching and in all administration to the extent that it has been in social work education and practice. There is a need for the learner to receive help, a need engendered by the nature of professional learning and perhaps peculiarly by the nature of social work. In this paper I have chosen to concentrate on the young adult who is having his first experience in social work, although he may have had employment that has tested his interest and aptitude. With this group, I specify some of the needs which create problems in learning which make help by supervisors necessary.

The social work student begins practice before he has knowledge essential for competent performance. Even when he has knowledge, practice begins before he has assimilated it. The need for help, therefore, is created by the discrepancy between demands and capacity to perform. Furthermore, it is created by the discrepancy between

---

* Published in *The Social Service Review*, Vol. XXXVII, No. 4, December, 1963.
[1] In the United States in recent years, student supervisors have been designated 'field work instructors', a practice which had the purpose of confronting them with their responsibility to teach through emphasizing their identity as educators. The author has chosen to retain the title 'supervisor' because it follows through on a previous paper (*ibid.*), in which the administrative identity of the supervisor is emphasized. It is the pressure of this identity which often precipitates students' need for help. Also, the full-fledged performance of this function often is a means to help students accept and use the supervisor as teacher and helper. Therefore, the term 'supervisor' gives prominence to the interplay of the three functions rather than to one.

demands and personality development implicit in performance capacity. When the integrative task exceeds integrative capacity, the learner often erects defences against anxiety which impede rather than support learning. Hence there arises the need for individualized help to safeguard the potential for emotional-intellectual integration essential for the mastery of knowledge. When knowledge possesses the learner rather than being possessed by him, it bedevils him, producing uncertainty and confusion. Knowledge relevant to social work practice is amassed at rapid tempo so that inevitably there is a problem in integration. Until he can make the new knowledge his own, the student is not free to use it effectively.

Social work educators become attentive to the part played by the emotions in professional learning and to social work education as a means to personality growth and change essential for the conduct of social work's helping processes. They attempted to teach in ways that would help the learner hold together his knowing, thinking, feeling and doing as he moved through the educational experience. Such teaching called for attention to the individual differences in learners. The problem of fostering emotional-intellectual integration led to wide swings in emphasis on the priority of knowledge versus the priority of fostering emotional readiness to learn. The push to individualize led to individualization of a kind and degree which did not prepare the student for demands of practice. Some of us recall the period of passivity, when we awaited the student's psychological readiness. Supervisors, in soft-pedalling their administrative function, withheld criticism and in many ways did not hold the student as strictly accountable as was desirable for the welfare of the client or for his own development. In so doing, they provoked an ascending spiral of frustration, resentment and anxiety and thus fostered defences needlessly. Supervisors, having depreciated their teaching and administering functions, thereby became overworked helpers. They were pushed into becoming therapists, and the line between help appropriate to the educational situation and therapy was crashed. Perhaps because the student's need for help was heavy, a transference neurosis occurred because the relationship was felt as repetitive of earlier relationships in which one was helpless. We no longer have the cult of passivity to create this problem, but one still does find supervisors who operate this way, perhaps because they experienced this kind of supervision, or because for varied reasons they are not secure in their responsibility roles of teacher and sub-administrator.

It is clear today that individualization fails of its aims when it waives the reality demands of practice. Yesterday we were caught in the long-standing educational controversy about whether one emphasizes maturation and awaits readiness or whether one emphasizes nurture and anticipates maturation to stimulate readiness. It has become clear that the profession's demands, rather than the student's stage of maturation, must dicatate our timing. Herein lies some of the stress of social work education. These demands force us to postulate readiness, at least a potential within the student to master, with help, the stress created by discrepancy. While the demands of professional education cannot be individualized, the student can and must be individualized throughout the educational process. When an educational system processes its students without individualizing them, it becomes mechanistic and fails to afford a humanizing experience. The student is prepared for a professional life that becomes more treadmill than pilgrimage. Briefly, we emphasize nurture and anticipate maturation to stimulate readiness. What nurture? The nurture implicit in meeting valid dependency freely through teaching and helping the student find what he needs to know in order to be competent in a given situation, the nurture implicit in holding him accountable and in helping him hold himself accountable. The therapeutic attitude is to regard a student as educable until we learn that he is not. One therefore assumes a potential to cope with the reality principle—the welfare of the client. One does not waive demands, but helps the student meet them to the extent possible. We afford him a relationship oriented to current reality on the assumption that he can use it.

We must be clear about the essential difference between re-educational help in social work education and therapy. A teaching situation differs from a psychotherapeutic session, a class from a group therapy session, in its heavy reliance upon the student's capacity to experience change in feeling and thereby change in thinking through an intellectual approach. In professional education, both in classroom and in field work, the initial approach or attack is upon the intellect. Although the feelings provoked are of primary importance in determining what the person learns and whether or not he is able to learn, feelings are given a secondary place, in the sense that our concern is with the student's responses to educational content and to the demands of practice. In short, we teach and we administer and deal with the responses of the learner. The demand to think cannot be nicely timed to the individual's psychological readiness, as it may be in therapy, in which thinking is fostered as feelings are expressed, released, understood and changed.

In a professional school, a student is assumed to be educable if he is admitted. An educable student is one who can stand up to a reality confrontation at the start, as implied in an intellectual approach and in the presentation of content without reference to his emotional or psychological readiness of the moment. One expects that the feeling provoked will not be so great and so involving of the total personality and basic conflicts that the student will be unable to deal with his feelings if given such individualized help as depicted in this paper. Today this help is supported by educational methods which facilitate integration. Some of us recall the day when supervisors were pushed into the therapist role in part out of unrealistic demands on students, implicit in unenlightened methods, methods which bespoke the administrators' and teachers' lack of understanding of the human as a learner.

The student's stage of maturation is often a basic factor. What are the ascendant needs of early adulthood, the common conflicts, the traits and abilities to be expected which have significance for the demands of social work? The individual is becoming more self-determining because he has the wherewithal for the management of his own affairs and because society has this expectancy of him and accords him this right within social limits. Furthermore, he has this expectancy of himself. Self-dependence and autonomy are valued goals in which he has so much at stake emotionally that frustration in the attainment of them readily gives rise to defences.

There is a high potential for the assumption of professional responsibility, along with a readiness to respond to the maturation push which these responsibilities entail. Now is the time to affirm and use these propensities to the extent that the profession's social limits permit. But often, newly emancipated as the student is, authority-dependency conflicts persist or their residuals are readily activated. Moreover, the individual tutorial sessions to which he is subjected through a mandatory supervisory system frequently activate these conflicts, to produce resistance to supervision. The student's responses suggest such questioning protests as: 'Why am I not accorded the freedom I had in college, and in other jobs, to do as I see fit and to risk myself? Why am I not treated as an adult, with freedom to use my own head, to be a free-lancer, to experiment? Why is my intelligence mistrusted, and why must I do as others do rather than find my own ways of doing? Their tried and trusted ways are accomplishing no great results. I could not do much worse, and I might be less pedestrian in getting the client into action in solving his problems.' Out of the common tendency at this stage to project one's self onto the client, the novice is restive when his goals, felt, however, as the client's goals, are not attained promptly. The restiveness of the beginner with the slow movement and meagre results in many cases is well known.

The student, perceiving the implications in skilled helping, may feel inadequate and fearful of risking himself, but he feels even more inadequate and more fearful under the close scrutiny of that expert, the supervisor, who will see what a 'goofer' he is. And so, blocked in risking himself, he may anxiously withhold himself. Without help he would become a protective learner, one who would exact meticulous instruction and use it warily with the aim of self-protection. As his frustration engenders hostility towards the supervisor whom he fears, he may distort his instructions. In so doing he is risking what the supervisor gave him, not himself, with the unconscious purpose of defeating him.

Resistance stemming from dependency-authority conflicts takes innumerable forms, but the fact remains that the social limits of the profession dictate that the client's welfare be put first. Therefore the student must come to peace with supervision, whatever his initial feelings about it. His concept of himself as supervisee and his concept of supervision which involves his concept of the supervisor must undergo change. The supervisor's helping function frequently comes into play in enabling the student to effect the change in feeling about supervision essential for modification of thinking and doing.

The following situation illustrates how these conflicts may be seen in beginning practice:

Miss A, aged 22, a trainee in an in-service training programme, during her first month in training had bungled two cases through not seeking supervisory help, despite the fact that her obligation to use supervision had been made known. Following the first episode, she had been confronted with the demand that she seek instruction. She had remorsefully acknowledged her sin of omission, but shortly thereafter had repeated it. She was quick to condemn herself and seemed truly concerned about her behaviour.

In the supervisory session that followed, she was tense but characteristically took responsibility for opening the interview. In a challenging manner, she said, 'Well, I certainly messed up that case.' The supervisor, acknowledging that the consequences had not been helpful to the client, commented also that the student had seemed so concerned about these consequences that she had immediately sought help as she recognized her mistakes. The student interrupted to exclaim, 'You are about to say my timing is bad!' after which the supervisor asked her what she thought. She replied that she just did not understand it herself. The supervisor said she had wondered whether she had been as helpful to the student as she might have been. Perhaps there was some reason why the student had felt the need to proceed alone, even though she must have recognized that she was on unfamiliar ground. The student's apprehensive manner gave way to a look of relief, and she talked freely. (The student had anticipated condemnation; instead, the supervisor conveyed her intent to understand—and in proffering a dispassionate appraisal of what was wrong, she engaged the student in problem-solving.)

The student said she had just seemed to barge in. She described the pressure that the client had brought on her for an immediate solution to her problem. She had felt she must do something quickly because the client was upset and unhappy. The supervisor acknowledged that it was good that she wanted to help the client—that this desire is fundamental in all social work—but added that sometimes in our eagerness to be helpful we give in to pressure and then cannot be helpful without help. (The supervisor affirmed that which can well be cherished—the helping impulse—but pointed out its limitations and the student's need for help.) The student said quickly: 'That's what I did—failed to help. I kept thinking last night about how I really got that woman into trouble, and I could not sleep'.

The supervisor commented that some mistakes are inevitable; we expect them. Furthermore, we probably could learn the hard way out of our mistakes—they can be steps in learning—but whenever possible we should avoid them. The agency's responsibility for the welfare of the client does not permit us to let students or workers learn through mistakes than can be prevented by use of supervision. (The supervisor confronted the student with the reality demands of professional education and conveyed the basic reason for supervision.) The student was silent. She did not respond with a prompt 'Yes, yes', to the supervisor's rational approach in making known agency demands. Some students might have assented, thus conveying the readiness to conform not yet attained through facing one's feelings and misbehaviour. The student shortly volunteered that she was used to assuming responsibility. She spoke of having lost her mother at an early age, and of her father's placing responsibility upon her. Emphatically and zestfully she added, 'I like it—I like to make decisions and get things done'. (Note that she is implying 'You do not understand *me* and my ways—the kind of person I am.' Also note the self-assertion, 'Let me be as I am.') The supervisor commented, 'I can see you do', and again pointed out the limitation of what she brings in this respect. In response to this, the student enquired, 'Why do you think I did as I did in that last case?' This self-inquiry was raised not provocatively, but showing concern. (A bid for understanding in order to understand herself?)

The supervisor asked her to try to reconstruct what her reasoning had been. (Note that she omits what her feeling had been.) The student replied that she knew she had been dealing with material on which she had no information. She knew that the supervisor was just across the hall, that she had always been generous with her time. The supervisor suggested that it was something other than reluctance to bother the supervisor that had prevented her from seeking help. The student nodded her head in affirmation, but said, 'I just don't understand it, that's all'. She lapsed into silence.

The supervisor broke the silence with the comment that perhaps the student had some negative feelings about asking for help, that she was made uncomfortable by asking, that she felt she should know all the answers herself even though she was a beginner. The student reflected on this, then said, slowly, 'I've always made good grades in school'. The supervisor explored the relevance of this. The student appeared puzzled, then added: 'I was just thinking about what you said, and then I remembered how important it has always been for me to be the outstanding student. My father was superintendent of schools, and everyone expected me to know all the answers. I was in agony at school if I was called on and couldn't come up with the right answer.' The supervisor commented that these feelings must have been burdensome to her and that this perhaps was something to think about further if they persisted, adding that no one expected her to have all the answers in her work here for some time. She pointed out that in both cases on which she had had difficulty there were procedures not covered in the orientation sessions or in supervisory sessions. (Note that the supervisor proffered her a departure from her past and thereby opened the door to a corrective experience.)

The student commented that if the supervisor had washed her hands of her today she would have had it coming, adding, with a sigh of relief, 'I just couldn't stand to fail in my work.' The supervisor replied that her work showed promise. The session closed with the reassurance that the next session would be devoted to an appraisal of wherein it did and wherein she needed help.

The sequel—After this conference the student engaged in over-use of the supervisor, asking help repetitively. (Note the reaction formation against her impulses—for equilibrium and for the mastery of a problem). As her unnecessary use of the supervisor was identified, this response tapered off, and she progressively showed ability to differentiate between matters which she could handle independently and those which she could not. In the course of the year there was still question about her ability to control her impatience for results. This was not so extreme that the supervisor questioned her potential for casework. (One notes here the projection of her life-situation into her work—a repetition of the past in that what has been demanded of her she demands of others, a propensity with which she may need further help or which she may outgrow).

Appraisal and prognosis—In this instance, the supervisor encountered a student with authority-dependency conflicts typical of the young adult. She brought to the educational experience a high expectancy of success and a high expectancy of herself with anxiety about measuring-up. She suffered the burden of competing, not only with others, but also with herself. Lacking knowledge and skill for independent functioning, she handled her feelings of inadequacy by doing on her own, by denying the dependency implicit in learning. In this behaviour she used an established pattern determined by demands made on her in the past and by self-inflicted demands— namely, that she as her father's daughter must know all the answers, must succeed, and perhaps also must equal her mother, whom she to some extent replaced in the life of the father. The supervisor probably had mother values. One suspects transference elements here, therefore resistance to help from the supervisor. If this had been a profound problem, the student might have continued to need to rival the supervisor and to be able to get along without her. Her response to help probably would not have been as ready.

It is noteworthy that the supervisor did not explore the past familial situation thrust at her by the student. Had she confused the role of educator with that of therapist, she probably would have done so. Instead, she proffered a helping relationship corrective of the past, and relied on this to enable the student to use help. The student's response does not negate the possibility of deeper psychological implications, but it does argue that the student is sufficiently unentangled in the past to use current relationships realistically and to regulate her own behaviour.

As one looks to the future one sees the following dynamic determinants which may enable the student to become a helper rather than a pusher: Her desire to succeed may motivate identification with the profession so that as she acts professionally she may mature, through being nurtured for growth. But the vital dynamics in change will be her concern for the consequences to the client. The unanswered question still is the extent of her capacity for object-love as compared with self-love, her capacity to meet the needs of others as compared with need for self-maximation and the meeting of her own need. To the extent that these capacities outweigh her self-centred needs, there will be a potential for growth through her experience in social work. Should the reverse be the case—and her propensity to push clients constitute a problem for them and for her professional development—she will need further help. In that event the supervisor would continue to focus on the consequence to the client as the means to motivate change. If the student cannot respond to this, her past rigidly persisting in the present would be defined as a problem requiring help other than what the supervisor can give—i.e., therapy.

This situation has been cited in illustration of authority-dependency conflicts as a source of difficulty in professional education. It illustrates also two other problems often implicit in the student's stage of maturation. The first of these has to do with giving and taking.

Adult responsibilities are not shouldered lightly by mature young adults. The stress of preparation for life-work is frequently accompanied by other stresses implicit in becoming adult. Normally this is a somewhat anxious, self-centred period when the individual is absorbed in getting his own life under way. In entering social work he is drawn concurrently into helping others set their lives straight.

A major struggle confronts him in the light of the central conflict of this period—that of 'intimacy versus isolation'. Erik Erikson holds that the mastery of intimacy is a major struggle now.[1] This implies mastery of the fear of ego loss so that relationships may be not only sustained but experienced fully and freely without erection of defences which constrict or distort them. Fear of ego loss occurs in situations that call for self-abandon. The social worker comes up against many a personal and social situation which cries out to him to give fully,

[1] *Childhood and Society*, W. W. Norton & Co., New York, 1950, pp. 229–31.

freely and with depth of feeling. It may be difficult to do so without getting lost, confused and entangled in the giving. Who am I, myself or my client? The threat of loss of self-identity compels self-questioning and, in some instances, the defence of retreat into self.

Experienced supervisors perceive that the problem is that of over-identification versus repudiation. Self-abandon alternates with self-restraint. Caught in this conflict, students cope with themselves variously. Some swing back and forth between these extremes; others are more consistently inclined to one or the other—over-identification, with abandonment of self, or weak identification out of self-restraint. A common defence against loss of self-identity in the helping relationship is to try to make the client over in one's own image through projection of one's own values and goals onto him. Or there may be the reverse of this self-assertion: self-negation may occur. Empathy may push the worker to permit the client to project his values, his problematic concerns, upon the worker to an extent that the worker is helpless because he feels like the client rather than with him. A reaction against this propensity may follow as the student tries to extricate himself. He may retaliate through self-assertive projection of himself onto the client or may repudiate him through withdrawal. His motivation to help breaks down in the face of discouraging outcome, and he gives up the struggle. Students who invest themselves deeply out of strong feeling for troubled people are prone to let the client engulf them. The potential for object-love, the strong motivation to serve, often implies an ability to put the client's welfare first, once the student is helped to regulate his own feelings and needs in the give-and-take of the helping relationship. Sometimes the self-assertive student is more difficult to help, as his own need for self-identity and self-maximation may engender defences against identification with troubled people. He cannot risk finding himself in losing himself. In these instances, narcissistic ego and constricted personality sometimes operate against the making of a full-fledged social worker, in whom the motivation to serve must outweigh self-centred aims.

The problem of over-identification occurs with high frequency in the educable social worker. Supervisors will find the reading of Virginia Robinson's portrayal of Jessie Taft a rewarding experience as a study of the growth and development of a true learner.[1] In her early years she was prone to over-identification and self-abandon in giving. What

[1] Virginia P. Robinson, *Jessie Taft—Therapist and Social Work Educator: A Professional Biography*, University of Pennsylvania Press, Philadelphia, 1962, Part II, pp. 41–63, specifically p. 48.

motivated her to regulate this propensity? The same qualities of heart and mind which motivates students today to use the supervisor's help in the regulation of their needs—her readiness to look at what she was doing to her clients, her discomfort over failing them. The student who is self-centred and self-concerned will be more defensive about the use of this help. He will be more prone to project his failure. He will find it difficult to make learning a conscious process. He may become a self-conscious worker rather than one ever ready to become conscious of self in the sense of looking objectively at himself in the client's response to him.

In early adulthood, as the individual enters social work, his problem commonly and normally is that of giving and taking, of giving and withholding. The mature individual gives all that he has to give on occasion, but discriminative giving rather than measured giving, which protects the giver, must become a pattern. Many students will need individualized help in making the need and capacity of others the measure of their giving and of their withholding.

Other problems stem from the persistence of the past in the present. At this stage of life the student is more vulnerable than he may be later to experiences which activate his past. He may still cling to cherished values as he evaluates others. Specific incidents or demands or knowledge may revive past painful experiences or ineptitudes. The latter may become repetitive trauma, provoking emotional response that may be exceptionally stressful and may call for help that the supervisor cannot give. Whether he needs help may be contingent on the extent to which he survived the earlier stress—that is, whether it impeded growth or contributed to growth despite some cost to the personality. Of decisive importance is the extent to which the individual is accessible to experiences and relationships that correct the past. For example: A student may reveal marked anxiety in trying to help a client who rejects her child. Her hostility towards this mother causes her to swing back and forth between the expression of punitive attitudes in the withholding of help, to opposite behaviour in which she must correct her professional misdemeanours through permissive attitudes and giving excessive help. From all this student says and does, the supervisor is reasonably certain that she is undergoing a repetitive experience that is painful and confusing. He does not explore the student's early experience in her relationship with her own mother. He focuses instead on eliciting and understanding the student's feelings about this mother. He shows understanding of her anger and dislike. He directs her to consider how this woman came to feel and act as she does, and he holds the student accountable to try to understand and to meet this woman's need, regardless of whether or not she feels kindly towards her. He grants that the woman's behaviour is unacceptable, but he holds that the woman herself is to be accepted and understood and helped. As the student sees and feels that this mother fails her child out of having been failed in her own relationships, the student becomes less aligned with the child versus the mother She begins to feel with the mother and, as the mother responds positively, making more productive use of help, the student is able to fulfil her professional responsibility.

In this instance the student subsequently made brief comments which showed insight gains—to the effect that she had a hard time not projecting her own experience, but she was working at it. The supervisor did not explore to elicit the specifics in her own past. Since she was able to be confronted and to confront herself with her learning problem and achieve mastery of it, the supervisor relied on the therapy implicit in the educational experience progressively to correct the past. As in the case of Miss A, an important clue to her probable ability to use help lay in her ambivalent behaviour towards this woman—out of strong motivation to behave professionally, and her discomfort over failing her. As guilt and hostility were lowered through the supervisor's help, she could permit herself insight.

I cite one more supervisory situation, one in which a complex of problems and more total involvement of the personality might have made the line between re-education and therapy difficult to hold, had the supervisor not had the skill he brought into helping.

Mr J, age 24, was admitted to second-year field work conditionally, when it was difficult to assess his unsatisfactory performance the first year because of objective factors which had made for an unrealistic demand. His first-year placement had been in an experimental group in a psychiatric hospital where he had a difficult caseload of seriously disturbed patients whose relatives posed a large task for a beginner. There had been a change in supervisors at the end of seven weeks from an experienced woman supervisor to whom, however, he could not talk freely because he found it difficult to talk to women, to a young man with no previous supervisory experience, with less casework experience, and with no experience in this setting. It was clear that the supervisor had been insecure in his role as teacher and helper and seemingly therefore overactive as a didactic teacher and hesitant as a helper. The student saw himself, retrospectively, as having over-identified with his patients when he felt the supervisor's limitations and could not turn to him for help. At the time, he attributed his own poor performance to his own problems, and he suffered much anxiety in feeling that he, like his patients, was mentally or emotionally ill.

Academically his work had been satisfactory, but he had become increasingly withdrawn in class discussion. He used his faculty adviser only when she initiated conferences, and he denied any difficulty in field work. The assessment of the first year was that the persistence of his past in the present indicated a neurosis. In his work with clients, the student revealed a fear of hostility, a fear of relationships with women, and an inner absorption which depleted his energy and limited his ability to relate to the needs of others. Her personalized his clients' initial resistance and withdrew rather than helping them express their anxiety. He pervasively recreated his family's conflict in his work with clients. This appraisal confronted the school with a discouraging picture suggestive of pathology. The question remained: to what extent was this a situational neurosis or a character neurosis? Not to be ignored was the fact that in his retreat from helping and being helped the student was repeating his supervisor's retreat from that function.

To his second-year supervisor in a family agency, it was clear that the student from the start must separate the two experiences, must have a new beginning. In the initial conference the supervisor functioned as follows:

The supervisor encouraged Mr J to talk about past experiences that had been successful and gratifying. This interview provided data for tentative evaluation of his initial motivation and enabled the supervisor to help him reclarify and assert his wish for professional achievement. It enabled the student to share his feelings of discouragement and afforded the supervisor information about what had been emotionally disturbing.

The supervisor made known some of the demands in his first-year caseload which required more skill than might be expected of a first-year student. The discussion relieved the student's feeling of failure and prompted him to volunteer that his difficulties were heightened by problems in supervision. He described in some detail what he felt had happened to him to affect his use of supervision. Although there was some bitterness and rationalization, there was not excessive projection. The supervisor used this discussion to make known that he would be working differently with him and that he was ready to accept responsibility to help him in areas in which he had felt

K

deprived. As the student blamed himself inordinately, the supervisor tried to reverse the pattern of self-recrimination by injecting the realities he was ignoring. Reality was also introduced to correct his distorted fears of the faculty.

No attempt was made to discourage personal remarks about his parents. These were not explored in depth, but the supervisor indicated that they had interest in relation to his motivation for social work. He attempted to enhance the student's wish to learn, by clarifying that, in spite of difficulties, he seemed determined to become a social worker. When he asserted this wish, the supervisor clarified mutual expectancies in the supervisory relationship.

The supervisor explored the student's feeling about agency assignment, because of the feelings students have about lack of choice. There was opportunity for him to consider his motivation in relation to a family agency. This was not clarified until later, when he revealed his unrealistic expectation that he would be dealing largely with requests for concrete services and less with problems in relationships having emotional content.

At the close of the initial conference, the supervisor focused on immediate tasks by outlining the kinds of cases the student would be expected to carry and selecting the specifics of the policy manual that would be of immediate concern to him. The supervisor also suggested questions to focus the study of two cases assinged. In this he was attempting to partialize the task in order to protect the student from feeling overwhelmed with the complexities of the new situation.

In his introduction to the second year, the new beginning was marked by the prominence given to the supervisor's helping function, the performance of which the previous supervisor had abdicated. The administrative function was highlighted in making known demands, in the assignment of responsibilities, and in making known certain expectations.

Subsequently the supervisor for a period gave time freely to convey interest and direction in learning. However, he maintained a task-centred focus. Consequently, when the student described his personal problems and expressed a feeling of hopelessness, the supervisor heard him out and accepted his feelings but then related these discussions to case situations. Discussion of case situations involved considerable clarification of what was inherent in the case and what Mr J was projecting into it. This sorting out of the objective and subjective sharpened his perception of his own anxieties.

Accompanying this there was open discussion of his problems in case management as they emerged more clearly, in his fear of hostility and rejection, his anger towards clients. In these discussions the student related his learning problems to personal fears and life-patterns. At the close of a month the student reported with elation that he had arranged for psychiatric treatment.

The supervisor had some anxiety that his tempo had been too fast, that he might have precipitated Mr J's treatment. If so, he feared that the precipitous decision might mean a retreat from learning, but the student did not use his treatment defensively. In fact, his social work performance improved progressively. The supervisor recalled that before this self-referral to a psychiatrist there had been several discussions in which he had attempted to enhance the student's respect for the courage and potential maturity involved in the client's seeking help. Apparently this discussion was incorporated and used by the student in his own behalf. At the close of the year he showed promise as a social worker, so that the school had no reservations in recommending him for employment.

One sees here a situation in which a supervisor in the context of a supportive relationship oriented his three-fold function of teaching, helping and administering to the student's need without waiving reality demands. Because the supervisor gave him help in seeing himself in his work, the student saw much that simultaneously heightened both his discomfort and his ability to cope with himself. Undeniably the supervisor's activity pushed the student into therapy. The student needed and wanted more relief from his discomfort over his problematic professional performance than he could obtain from the supervisor. Thus he became motivated to get help elsewhere, but, because the supervisor had helped him, he had hope and confidence that he could be helped. This hope the supervisor affirmed in making 'taking help' ego-challenging rather than ego-deflating. This is a good example of an educational relationship which served as a therapeutic one.

Whether his difficulties are rooted in unresolved authority-dependency conflicts, in intimacy-versus-isolation conflicts, in attachments to the past, or in other sources, it is probable that the student is feeling stress. The nature and extent of his feeling, as well as both his capacity to cope with his feeling and his ways of coping, will determine the size of his integrative task. These factors will determine also the nature and extent of the help he needs and his response to it. It is common for students under stress to deny their feelings out of discomfort and out of fear. Reared in a scientific age, students may draw on their misconception of the scientist's schooled feeling. The protective ego often whispers, 'To be objective professionally one must not feel.' This is an unhappy solution for many reasons. Denial of feeling will desensitize the student. It will constrict him in relating to people and lead to emotional shallowness. It will impede his identification with social work as a helping profession. It is as the student's relationships gain emotional depth that acculturation to the mores and demands of social work occurs. Furthermore, it is to be remembered that freedom to feel makes for play of the mind and thereby contributes to creative intellectual functioning. His mentors in classroom and field work can well be concerned to free him to feel warmly and deeply. It is as he is free to feel that he becomes able to face and to regulate his feeling. He thereby is enabled to make conscious use of his feeling, that is, to express disagreement or withold it with appropriate reference to time, place and person. It is as his feelings are expressed and respected that he will be able to respect the feelings of others and come to see that 'as a man thinketh in his heart, so is he'. The dignity of man, his individuality, is contingent on the fusion of his feeling and his thinking.[1]

Space limitations have driven me to focus narrowly on the beginning stage of young adults. We encounter many older students, some with social work experience and all with more work experience. In some instances the authority-dependency conflicts, the problems in giving and taking, have been outgrown to the extent that the past has been outgrown, but often these problems are there, more masked now by the individual's defences against them. These defences may or may not be useful in social work. The demand for change therefore may be more threatening because it involves acceptance of the dependency and authority implicit in learning at an age when it may be even more difficult to be dependent and to be subjected to professional discipline. It may involve also the unlearning implicit in modification of well-entrenched behaviour and of social work practices in which the student has felt competent. Supervisory help is essential, however, even though in some ways and at times it is difficult for the supervisor and the student. The principles and means of helping are essentially the same. It is clear that the helping function of the supervisor is lowered when

---

[1] I recommend to all social workers the paper entitled 'Living and Feeling', by Jessie Taft, first published in *Child Study* in 1953 and now reprinted in her professional biography. Robinson, *op. cit.*, pp. 140–53.

educational and administrative methods bear the imprint of psycho-logical understanding—understanding of the learning process and of the stress implicit in the demands of social work education. Helpful methods aim to support the ego's adaptive capacity and to prevent the individual's overuse of its protective function. This summary will not include these methods. It will instead focus on methods and principles of helping when teaching and administrative methods have not fulfilled their aim, either because the student is unable to respond to them or because they have fallen short of good educational practice. Obviously, modification of method frequently is indicated to support the supervisor's function as helper. In this he is always dealing with a problem in learning, a problem in use of the opportunity to learn or a problematic response to reality demands.

The following must be kept in mind in helping the student:

1. The supervisor helps the student identify the problem or confronts him with it. Confrontation may precede the student's readiness; the needs of the client dictate the tempo.

2. The supervisor gives the student ample opportunity to delineate the problem as he sees it and feels it. The supervisor encourages and explores, so that he may explain the student's part in it and the part played by circumstance or other persons. He helps the student sort out both the subjective and the objective factors and forces.

3. The situation is then set up as a problem-solving one. What can the student do about it, and what can the supervisor do to help him perform more competently in the interest of the client?

4. In the process of reaching this point, the supervisor affirms what is acceptable and useful in the student's behaviour in the problematic situation but makes known the what and the why of that which is inappropriate. This may imply making known or clarifying agency demands and the demands of professional learning. Often it involves clarifying the supervisory relationship, if use of it is part of the problem.

5. In evoking and exploring feelings, the supervisor acknowledges and understands the student's feeling. He thus accepts the student himself but not necessarily his behaviour. The limitations of it are made known again with inclusion of why the behaviour is not useful or appropriate.

6. When, in exploring the problematic situation, the student blocks in recognizing the import of his part in it, the supervisor tentatively postulates probabilities—presenting them as what the import may be, what it seems to him, the supervisor, to be out of his experience with other students and workers with comparable difficulties. This may

provoke resistance which will then have to be dealt with. If blocking persists, the student is charged with the responsibility of trying to figure out for himself the import of his behaviour. Whether or not he is able to do this, the behaviour will have to change. Students at times have to be pushed to act in a way they do not feel. In so doing, they may come to feel differently. Furthermore, as they cope with themselves with some success, defences are lowered, thus permitting insight gains. Sometimes, contingent on the seriousness of the implications for the client, the student's inability to change will lead to consideration of his educability for social work and/or his need to get help elsewhere.

7. As the student is appraised negatively, he may well feel threatened by the resultant deflated concept of himself, how he looks both to himself and to the supervisor. It is important to use 'norms' of development in appraisal of lacks in performance and inappropriate attitudes and behaviour. Unrealistic expectancy of self or of others is unjust and ego-deflating. It can lower motivation. If he feels that he has not fallen below realistic expectancy, the student's sense of failure is diminished so that he may be enabled to work on the problem. Norms must not be used invalidly, for false reassurance is not helpful. When a student is not coming up to norms, the reasons should be ascertained to the extent possible and efforts should be made to assess what he can do about it or what the supervisor can help him do.

8. When the student places his difficulties in the past, the supervisor does not immediately explore the past, but makes known the difference, with the hope that the student may be able to use the current experience to correct the past through being able to separate the two. But if his use of the past to explain his difficulties persists, the supervisor may explore it, though not deeply or extensively. Some exploration is important in order to see its relevance to the present for use in helping the student relate to his current work performance.

9. As implied throughout the preceding description, a good deal inevitably happens to make learning a conscious process and to help the student become conscious of himself in order to regulate his use of himself as a social worker. Normally, students gain insight as anxieties are lowered and defences relax. They often will spontaneously verbalize insight and often use it, whether or not they put it into words.

10. Finally, the student-supervisor relationship should not be a one-to-one relationship but a two-some in which the two as one are continuously related to the agency and the client. This relationship has been set up to serve the agency on behalf of the client; therefore, these are kept in focus—as the reality principle. As this occurs, student

and supervisor do not become absorbed to an entangling degree in one another. The issue of controlling and being controlled disappears. As they work together, the student's capacity to put the client's needs and wants before his own and to use the agency and supervision for the client rather than for self-maximation will become the dynamic factor in his use of help. If the student is not motivated by concern for the client, it is probable that his personal needs call for a help of a kind beyond the scope of agency supervision. Concern for the client's welfare and concern for his own professional competence motivate change, given the capacity to change. They therefore are the major criteria of a student's educability.

10

THE FIELDWORK SUPERVISOR
AS EDUCATOR*

LOLA SELBY

TEACHING is a primary responsibility of the field work supervisor, and field work is a course in the curriculum just as casework or social administration are courses—but with some differences to be elaborated later. It is impossible to discuss field work teaching without also discussing the development of social work education, because supervised field work has always been a part of formal training for social work. Supervised experience in an agency, however, has not always had the same connotation in the educational programme that it holds today.

American social work literature tells us that earlier education for social work practice really represented vocational training for specific agency tasks under specific agency auspices. It was a form of apprenticeship training, carried on in agencies, with experienced practitioners taking over responsibility for helping the inexperienced to 'learn the trade'. New workers in an agency were taught 'how to do' by being shown and told by those who knew 'how to do'. New workers learned defined tasks and procedures by doing them under supervision. The emphasis was on the doing, and the supervisor saw to it that the doing was according to the rules and accepted practices. The supervisor's job was more administrative than educational; indeed, the root meaning of the word *supervisor* is *overseer*—'one who watches the work of another with responsibility for its quality'. The supervisor had the task of assigning a work load, and checking on the new worker's performance in order to determine if he or she was abiding by the rules and procedures of the agency; and the supervisor was the one to whom the worker came for decisions regarding the giving of a specific service. Not until some time later did the decision-making include discussion of 'treatment plans'. This later stage of development in the U.S.A. followed the introduction of Mary Richmond's 1917

* A talk given at a Week-End Course for Supervisors (University of Birmingham, England), April, 1962.

formulation of casework activity as 'study, diagnosis and treatment'. When the supervisor undertook some responsibility for helping the worker with these steps, the supervisor became a teacher of casework methodology, as well as an overseer.

In the early days, social work was not yet recognized as a profession, but was considered to be a job or a vocation, hence it was natural that training for social work began as apprenticeship training. It is a matter of consequence, however, that there was this kind of beginning, because from the start a field work experience was seen to have a place in the scheme of things. In the United States this early pattern of training was soon reinforced by the educational philosophy of John Dewey which had much influence on American educational practice when it was introduced in the early part of the 20th century. Dewey's theory, 'Learn by doing', fitted neatly with the social worker's concept of practice as a way of acquiring skill in the carrying out of agency responsibilities and tasks. That a practice has validity in social work education has never seriously been questioned by social workers, even though question has been raised about the length of time necessary for such experience to take hold, and also question as to whether some of the traditional patterns of field work experience might be modified.

Formal social work education in the U.S.A. began as a summer training course for Charity Organization Society workers employed by the New York C.O.S. This was in 1898. By 1904 this programme had developed into a one-year training course under the New York School of Philanthropy (now the Columbia School of Social Work) and this pattern rapidly spread throughout the country. Almost from the beginning, formal social work training in the United States became attached to universities, so that quite early such training began to move away from straight apprenticeship training under the direction of specific agencies. In both Britain and America, however, the field work supervisor has been an important personage since the beginning in social work training, but his or her responsibilities have changed somewhat as the concept of professional education has developed.

Social work literature on the subject of supervision has much to say about the three-fold function of the present-day supervisor—administrative, helping and teaching. I have already noted that the first supervisors were really 'overseers' in the administrative sense, supervising an apprentice in the learning of a craft. This phase (in America at least) was followed by what Charlotte Towle calls the 'relationship phase', when the helping function of the supervisor was emphasized above all else. During this period supervisors had a hard time distingushing between supervision and therapy in their work with staff or students. The last decade or so in America (and also to some extent in Britain) has brought an emphasis on the teaching functions of the field work supervisor, so we may now say we are in the 'educational phase'. At the present time, however, we recognize that administraion, helping and teaching all have a place in the supervisor's responsibilities, and that they are closely related. If this article seems to over-emphasize the educational responsibilities at the expense of the other two, it is only because time does not permit coverage of everything related to supervision, and because supervising students in field work places some priority on the educational function. All three functional aspects of supervision still have a bearing on the field work programme, and are linked closely in the supervisory method of instruction. For instance, the field work supervisor must exercise his *administrative* function in holding the student to account for a certain quantity and quality of production; in implementing that production by providing learning and practice opportunities (which take some administrative planning); in seeing that service to clients is adequately rendered with agency regulations and procedures properly carried out; in planning the field work courses, etc., with the agency and school. The field work supervisor must employ his *helping* function by supporting and sustaining the student in times of stress, by providing a positive climate for learning, by managing the supervisory relationship in a professional helping way, by making use of what he knows about people and their behaviour in work with students, by helping students to identify and modify feelings and other obstacles which are impeding their progress. As a *teacher* the supervisor makes use of what he knows about learning theory and learning behaviour; he gives of his knowledge, stimulates thinking, leads out with new ideas, holds students to grappling with ideas, encourages conscious thinking processes, gives students the opportunity to discuss their work and appraise it, to arrive at decisions, and to learn helping skills. The field work supervisor is also an educator when he plans teaching material, utilizes various methods of instruction and learning resources within the agency, provides a well-organized learning experience for his students, and uses the evaluation report session as an educational as well as an administrative tool.

There has been much thinking by American social work educators in recent years about curriculum planning, and about the whole gamut of social work education as an educational experience. Much of this thinking has been put forward by Charlotte Towle in her monumental volume, *The Learner in Education for the Professions.*[1] Her thinking about social work education has been influenced not only by what she and other social workers knew about people and learning processes from social work experience and from psychiatric understanding, but also by the philosophy of education represented by the writings of Dewey, Tyler and other educational theorists. The educational theory of Dr Ralph Tyler, former chairman of the Department of Education at the University of Chicago, then Dean of its Division of Social Sciences, and now connected with the Institute of Behavioral Sciences at Stanford University, has had considerable influence on curriculum planning in social work education in the United States since the early 1950s. This applies especially to what he has to say about the tasks in planning and conducting an educational programme. He lists the tasks as: (a) deciding on the objectives; (b) selecting learning experiences that will contribute to the objectives; (c) organizing the learning experiences to maximize their cumulative effect; (d) evaluating the effectiveness of the educational programme in attaining its objectives through appraising the educational progress of students. He points out that education is a process for changing the behaviour of students in desired directions—behaviour being used in the broad sense to include thinking, feeling and acting. When a student is educated he acquires ideas, habits, attitudes, interests, ways of thinking and professional skills which he did not have before; his behaviour has been changed. Hence the educational objectives have to do with the behaviour patterns that the educational establishment tries to develop in the student. The knowledge, skill and ways of thinking and doing that the student is expected to acquire are examples of these objectives. The only rational basis for selecting learning experinces and devising evaluation procedures is in terms of their relationship to the educational objectives.

Deciding upon educational objectives is not easy because it requires close thinking on the part of the educator. Classroom courses are much more effective, however, if they do reflect some such sense of direction, and field work courses too can be enhanced if subjected to similar planning. We used to think that the 'what' of casework, for instance, was taught in class, and the 'how' was pretty much taught in the field. It is now recognized that both the class and the field work offer opportunities for conceptual learning, and the job of the student supervisor has become increasingly similar to that of the classroom teacher in many ways. Field work supervisors, like classroom teachers,

[1] University of Chicago Press, Chicago, Illinois, 1954, Chap. 3.

introduce new knowledge as needed, and reinforce knowledge already acquired by the student. Field work supervisors can help students to generalize from specific case situations just as the classroom teacher does, and both field work and work in the classroom lead to the translation of theory into effective application. Field work carries a large share of the burden for helping the student to integrate his knowledge from the total curriculum because knowledge only comes to life as it is put to use.

We can say then that as an educator the field work supervisor is now considered to have responsibility for planning a field work course which, while having its own objectives and content, will be related to the total curriculum of the school and to the overall objectives of education for social work. The field work supervisor must develop teaching methods that will facilitate learning and that have an educational as well as a practice focus. The field work supervisor is responsible for helping the student to think in terms of concepts as well as in terms of a specific instance—the case—and to generalize from his learning in an individual case, so as to make his learning transferable. The field work supervisor has to consider the field work experience for a student in the light of what can realistically be learned by the student in a given period of time, what learning opportunities the agency offers, what order and progression of learning experiences will best implement the educational objectives. Individualized instruction is one of the chief assets of field work teaching, so the field work supervisor is expected to make use of the supervisory relationship in a sensitive way to enable the student to learn—and to enrich the supervisory sessions in every way possible. The field work supervisor is also expected to make use of other opportunities for student learning and teaching which can serve as a dynamic in the educational programme, through such educational opportunities as staff meetings, board meetings, conferences, visual aids and field visits.

Everything points to the need for the supervisor to use whatever he knows about learning theory, and what he can observe of students' learning patterns, in his work with students. Learning theory is not a topic easy to discuss, because with all the attention that has been given to the matter of learning and the educative process, psychologists and educators have not yet evolved a theory of learning that is universally accepted.[1] Hilgard points out that learning theories fall into two major families: the stimulus-response theories and the cognitive

---

[1] For a full discussion of current learning theory see Ernest R. Hilgard, *Theories of Learning*, N.Y., Appleton, Century, Crofts Inc., New York, 1956.

theories. The learning theories of the psycho-dynamicists, a third 'family', do not fall clearly in either of these two groups, but partake of them both.

The stimulus-response theorists believe that thinking is produced by some kind of chained muscular responses, and that what is learned can be called 'habit'. Habits are conditioned responses which in their highest form become smoothly operating skills. Theorists in the stimulus-response camp think that if the learned habits prove not to be appropriate in a given situation, the person attempts to reach an appropriate solution to the new problem by resorting to trial and error activity.

The cognitive theorists believe that thinking is related to central brain processes which involve memories and expectations, and that thinking processes involve goal-seeking behaviour. Instead of learning 'habits', the individual learns facts and 'alternate routes' of behaviour. Instead of trial and error learning, there is problem-solving by 'insight'. By this is meant that thinking is a kind of perceptual structuring of the 'problem' to be solved, with decision-making and action based on perception.

Nowadays most educators seem to prefer the cognitive theories to the stimulus-response theories to describe learning activity. Tyler, for instance, indicates that he does not see learning as being based on habit-formation, but rather on the process of generalization—applying principles to specific situations. But neither of these theories entirely satisfies the psycho-dynamic theorists. The latter consider thought processes to be influenced by the positive and negative values placed by the individual on his perceptions. The values stem from inner needs and drives, from cultural conditioning, etc. Learning and new ideas are seen as 'good' or 'bad' according to past experiences or according to the positive or negative values given to the perceptions. This is why the psycho-dynamicists say that learning has emotional elements. It is because of our interest in psycho-dynamics that we as social workers have become greatly concerned with the affective elements in learning —or with what Charlotte Towle refers to as the 'emotional elements in learning'. Her learning theory, given detailed elaboration in *The Learner in Education for the Professions*,[1] is based on a psycho-dynamic theory of personality development and personality integration —influenced chiefly by the ideas of such psychiatrists as Franz Alexander and Thomas French. She also finds congenial the cognitive theory of learning from generalizations and principles. She sees

[1] *Op. cit.*

learning as having the effect of reducing tension for some students and of arousing anxiety in others. She draws on psycho-analytic theory in speaking of the principle of inertia or economy which operates in learning. This principle has to do with man's characteristic attempt to achieve equilibrium and stability with a minimum of energy and effort. Despite this need to achieve equilibrium with a minimum of effort, the individual learns actively through activity. As Tyler says, 'In general, the learner learns only those things which he does'.[1] Hence learning takes place through the student's experience, through his reactions to the environment in which he is placed. In planning a field work course or any other course, therefore, it is necessary to decide on the educational experiences which should be provided, since it is through participating in these that learning will take place. Learning experiences involve students in feeling as well as in thinking. Both are important aspects of learning.

Charlotte Towle points out that emotions in large measure determine thinking and action (i.e. positive and negative values are given by the individual to his perceptions). Students bring strong feelings to the process of helping people and to the process of learning. These feelings will influence their work with clients, their use of supervision, their learning activity. Learning to be a social worker places heavy demands on the student's integrative capacities, because the integrative tasks are complicated and emotion-laden. There are some natural anxieties and fears inherent for the student in social work education. She lists the major anxieties as follows:

1. The fear of helplessness due to lack of knowledge and to the lag between newly acquired knowledge and the development of skill. (Fear related to high expectance of self, and/or out of concern for those served.)

2. Fear of the new by reason of its nature and meaning rather than fear of the newness itself. (Fear of change, not necessarily pervasive.)

   a. Experiences which threaten self-dependence.
   b. The demand to understand experience beyond one's own
   c. Responsibility to sustain consciousness of self, and to use the concept of the unconscious.

3. Dual intellectual processes (deductive and inductive), and multiple demands in the social work job.

Students, like everyone else, utilize defence mechanisms against anxiety.

---

[1] For a discussion of learning and learning experiences, see *Basic Principles of Curriculum and Instruction*, University of Chicago Press, Chicago, Illinois, 1950, prepared by Ralph W. Tyler, pp. 41–53.

Some anxiety is normal, and each student will express his anxiety in his own way. Most students will be able to respond to the learning situation with lessening anxiety: (1) providing the new learning does not run counter to deep emotional convictions which meet some deep emotional need, and (2) providing the relationship to the teacher is a positive one (if there is respect and trust rather than mistrust and fear). Most students have a strong impulse to learn, i.e. to grow, so with help there is forward movement. The supervisor has to become aware of the students' learning patterns and learning needs, in order to tailor the learning experiences to the individual situation.

Learning patterns is a term used to describe a student's characteristic ways of approaching and assimilating new experience. These patterns of learning are closely related to the individual's characteristic ways of handling the discomfort and stress imposed by the integrative task represented in learning. Ways of handling stress which prevent a free approach to new experience, and which inhibit change in feeling and thinking, may be called blocks to learning. Ways of handling stress in the learning situation which impede learning rather than assist it, often develop out of unresolved conflict over the dependency implicit in learning. Some young adults may find in the student role a re-creation of the emancipation problems they have so recently been struggling with in their push towards maturity. Some older students may find it difficult to take a student role because it makes them feel somewhat like children again or because they are afraid they cannot meet the expectations that the school holds for them as mature adults.

As a supervisor I have found it most interesting to note the differences in learning patterns of students, even to the differences in intellectual 'approach'. I will cite two examples from my experience in supervising students:

Student A stated as her goal in field work at the beginning of the year 'to find out what I really know about casework'. (This student had had prior work experience.) It soon became evident that she learned by doing rather than by what she termed 'thinking in advance'. Her learning had to be related to past or current experience to have meaning—otherwise it seemed 'academic' to her and was not fully absorbed. Student A had to learn about a case 'through the feel of it' (her terminology). She had to be 'in the case' before she could try to understand it. She felt lost in getting started in any kind of learning unless she could start with an experience. It was necessary, therefore, for her to plunge immediately into doing to relieve her anxiety. She arrived at formulations and generalizations after the doing—from the specific to the general (an inductive approach). She had to test all new ideas in practice before accepting them; they must 'feel' right to be acceptable. She was more comfortable with a specific experience than with a generalization—conceptualization was always hard work. It was easier for this student to operate intuitively than by consciously understood process, but this was balanced by a dogged persistence in pursuing new ideas until she was convinced she understood them.

Student B, by contrast, stated his goal in field work to be 'to learn just what a caseworker is supposed to do and how to do it'. This student had to learn initially via the intellect, by a very specific spelling out of content and theory. With this understanding the student gained courage to act. Without intellectual understanding of what was required and what to do, Student B was very pessimistic about his own ability to help people. He had to identify, interview by interview and case by case, the steps in casework activity, the dynamics, and what the client was trying to communicate—and then to consider appropriate responses. Once this student began to understand these things intellectually, the ideas could seep down and become a part of his emotional self. He was quite perceptive and sensitive when free of the anxiety of 'not knowing' or 'not understanding'. Student B always had to generalize before he could particularize (the deductive approach). Intellectual understanding freed him for doing, and with comfort in his understanding, he could permit himself some experimentation. This student was always able to analyse and synthesize with considerable facility.

Both of these students by pursuing their own individual ways of learning, intellectually and emotionally, were eventually able to achieve relative comfort in doing, and by the end of their field work assignment they had made definite progress. Understanding their learning pattern helped me, as the supervisor, to assits them in their learning and to recognize what was happening along the way.

I suggest that you make a study of your students' learning patterns, with a view to gearing your helping efforts to their individual needs.[1]

That there are stages in learning, soon becomes apparent to a field work supervisor as he gains perspective from having supervised a number of students. I know of no better discussion of these stages in

[1] For further exploration of this subject, see Sidney Berengarten, 'Identifying Learning Patterns of Students: An Exploratory Study', *The Social Service Review*, Vol. XXXI, No. 4, December, 1957.

learning for social work students than appears in the classic work of Bertha Reynolds, *Learning and Teaching in the Practice of Social Work*.[1] As a preamble to her description of the course of learning, she states: 'Learning to deal with new experiences involves paying attention to it'. The 'paying attention' often results in initial discomfort, but hopefully eventuates in mastery of the 'problem'. Reynolds lists the stages of learning as follows:

1. The stage of acute consciousness of self;
2. Sink or swim adaptation (a trial and error period);
3. The stage of understanding the situation without power to control one's activity in it (intellectual grasp);
4. Relative mastery, with both understanding and control of one's activity—i.e. skill in practice.

If we have some appreciation of differences in learning patterns, and of the stages in learning, we are in a better position to evaluate when a student's dependency is valid, or the reverse, when his independence is a sign of progress or vice versa, when a period of slowing down is 'normal' or a sign of trouble, when new learning should be introduced, when to help the student make his learning conscious, how to evaluate his production and help him to evaluate it.

Social work education inevitably involves the student in a significant personal and emotional growth experience. As has been pointed out in one book about social work education,[2] such education makes four demands on the learner—in knowing, feeling, being and doing. The social work student encountering these four demands must go through a process of personal reorganization in the development of his professional helping skills. As he begins to use himself in new ways in a helping role, as he develops increased self-awareness and understanding of others, and as he incorporates challenging new ideas from the curriculum, he experiences personal change through professional growth. Virginia Robinson refers to what occurs in this learning experience when she mentions 'the process of change, professionally initiated and limited', which becomes an organic growth process 'formed and directed by the unique nature of each individual self'.[3]

---

[1] Bertha Capen Reynolds, *Learning and Teaching in the Practice of Social Work*, Farrar and Rinehart, Inc., New York, 1942—see Chap. VII, 'Conscious Intelligence in Learning'.
[2] Ernest V. Hollis and Alice L. Taylor, *Social Work Education in the United States*, Columbia University Press, New York, 1951.
[3] Virginia P. Robinson, *The Dynamics of Supervision under Functional Controls*, Philadelphia, University of Pennsylvania Press, 1949.

Another social work educator, Bertha Reynolds, long ago made the statement that 'The dynamic of change, in either attitude or behaviour, lies in a relationship to a person'. In social work education students have opportunities to relate to their teachers both in the academic setting and in the field. Very often it is the field work supervisor who has the closest relationship with the student, because of the individualized teaching in the field, and because field work stimulates intense personal involvement on the part of the student. All the emotional elements of the student's learning come into play in the field work situation, and the supervisory method of teaching brings intensity of relationship into the foreground. The relationship factor, plus the provocative content of social work classroom and field material, naturally stimulates subjective reactions on the part of students. New insights about people and self, added to the supervisory relationship which may reactivate old authority-dependency conflicts or other basic conflicts, may impel the use of defence patterns for handling these conflicts, thereby inevitably arousing emotional response to the learning situation. The supervisor finds himself deeply involved in an interaction process which can lead both him and the student astray if he is not sure of his own role and responsibility. If the supervisor has come fresh from practice and has had little experience in student supervision, there is a tendency to become involved in a treatment way with students, and the educational focus becomes lost in the shuffle.

The supervisor has to hold firmly in mind the fact that his job is to focus on the student's professional development rather than on the student's personal needs and problems. If the student's personal difficulties are such that they have led him to seek therapy from the school rather than education, then the student should be encouraged to seek such help outside the school setting. The ultimate goal of the student's learning in the classroom and field work must always be kept in mind—self-assurance and independent functioning in the professional role and the ability to operate as a competent helper in the field of human relations without tripping over his own unconscious reactions, his personal value judgments or his defences.

A student's self-discovery within the context of learning how to become a social worker, may have therapeutic value for the student concerned, but it is basically an educational rather than a treatment experience. The field work supervisor is primarily an educator, and as such needs to clarify from the very beginning, as much through demonstration as through words, what the supervisory relationship is all about. The following aspects of the relationship need to be spelled out:

1. It is a working relationship—two people working together not to meet each other's personal needs, but to administer agency services helpfully to clients.

2. It is a professional relationship (teacher-learner) rather than a social one.

3. It is an interdependent relationship, with both parties having responsibilities, but different responsibilities.

4. The main purpose of the relationship is to help the student learn how to give service constructively, and to develop some social work skills.

With these points clarified, the supervisor is in a better position to focus on problems interfering with the student's learning, rather than on the student's emotional problems and emotional adjustment. Supervision is not a form of treatment, but is teaching in a helping way. The student's personal problems come within the province of discussion only as they may be interfering with the student's use of the educationl experience.

In his helping role, the supervisor uses the helping qualities of warmth, acceptance and support, creating a climate for learning that enables the student to discuss freely his questions, doubts, uncertainties, concerns as a learner. The supervisor, as a helper, shows respect for the student's ideas, and draws him into participation in the learning tasks. The supervisor uses his helping skills also in understanding the learner and helping the student identify learning problems. The supervisor has to translate what he knows about motivation, support, stimulation, acceptance, etc., from practice with clients to educational practice. Helping the student to define learning goals, to gain a sense of direction in his learning efforts, and to evaluate his own work and accomplishments is all a part of the supervisor's job. The student learns in contact with an alert, understanding supervisor, partly through identification with the supervisor who represents professional competence and partly as a result of being helped to make learning a conscious process.

The supervisor's administrative function has various aspects. The supervisor, as an agency representative, is ultimately responsible for seeing that the student carries out service to clients, observes the agency's rules and regulations, and works within agency function. A social worker as an agency representative is accountable to the agency and indirectly to the community. The student has to learn how to become a part of an agency staff, and the supervisor helps him in this by example, and by holding the student to account within the area of the student's defined responsibilities. The supervisor has a responsibility to help students learn such good work habits as promptness in recording, keeping appointments, organizing time productively, following necessary procedures. This kind of learning comes more easily if the supervisor can help the student to see purpose to administrative activity, understand the reasons behind agency policies and regulations, and appreciate constructive use of agency channels and organizational structure. This kind of learning is also easier if the student can be helped to see that administrative procedures can implement responsible service to clients. Often students initially see administrative procedures as limiting rather than implementing, or as red tape. The supervisor has to help the student to resolve his ambivalence about administration and its relationship to client's needs.

The supervisor cannot deny the authority element in the supervisory relationship. This authority element has to come into play when the supervisor holds the student to meeting his agency responsibilities, and in evaluation. The supervisor should not dodge negative comment when this is due. The student needs to know where he stands, and negative criticism can be helpful. The way it is given is the important thing. If the focus is not personal, but pointed toward the client's and the agency's need, and if the criticism is related to specific instance rather than generalized, it can be less condemning. If consideration can be given to what can be done to rectify or improve the problem situation, the student can perhaps move toward constructive change. Evaluation of work should, of course, be a continuous process related to the whole project of making learning conscious and helping the student to become able to look with some objectivity at his own work, to see what he is able to do well and in what areas he needs to strive for improvement.

The teaching responsibilities in supervision involve some formulation of teaching-learning objectives and these of course need to be worked out by the supervisor in close co-operation with the school so that greater integration between classroom and field learning can be achieved. The supervisor as teacher will help the student to link new knowledge with old knowledge, sift the relevant from the irrelevant, see the relatedness of facts, bring technical information to bear on practice, utilize both inductive and deductive reasoning in thinking about cases and case problems, analyse, synthesize and evaluate. It is helpful to give students some structure for looking at cases in the beginning, a simple structure like asking them to think about the material in relation to the following questions:

What the record indicates about:

—how the client got to the agency
—what the client is like as a person
—what he sees as his problem(s)
—how he seems to feel about his problem(s)
—what sort of help he wants from the agency
—what kind of help seems appropriate.

From such a simple but necessary organizing of thought about case material, the student can begin to formulate his own questions about the case to contribute to discussion in supervisory conference, and he can begin to consider ways and means of helping the client.

Supervisory teaching should concentrate on such essentials as understanding people and human behaviour, how agency purpose and the worker's helping role can be interpreted to clients, how clients can be drawn into participation in working on their problems, other aspects of casework method, including assessing the problem, canvassing alternatives and services available, and considering the client's goals. The supervisor should help the student to consider agency philosophy and focus, and how the particular agency relates to other agencies and welfare services in the communtiy. The supervisor should help the students to look at his cases as wholes as well as interview by interview, and to compare cases for likenesses and differences. He should help the student to derive some generalizations from specific instances for use in other situations. The supervisor should be well enough acquainted with the general content of what the student is getting in his classes at the school to provide field work experiences that will renforce the theoretical learning. While field work and classroom work cannot run parallel in every respect they must be closely related. The field work supervisor, like the classroom teacher, has to decide what to teach, how to teach it and in what order.

Work with each student has to be individualized, but there are a few principles related to supervisory method that are always essential to observe if the supervisory relationship is to serve its professional purpose. The following principles deserve priority:

(1) The supervisor should meet freely and adequately the valid dependency needs of the student, i.e. the need for help with learning

L*

whatever is necessary to fill the gap between where the learner is and the demands of his assignment.

(2) At the same time, the supervisor should encourage the student to be self-reliant in those areas where he has the necessary knowledge and competence to function independently.

(3) The supervisor should affirm the strengths the student brings but should not avoid helping him to face inadequacies in his performance.

(4) The supervisor should avoid making unrealistic demands on the student but should hold the student to meeting the reality demands of his responsibilities.

(5) The supervisor should help the student to focus on service to the client and on understanding the client and the client's needs and communications as a basis for appropriate helping activity.

(6) Remembering that early experiences set patterns, the first supervisory conferences should be planned to set the tone for the supervisor-student relationship with proper allocation of responsibilities between student and supervisor.

(7) The supervisor should arrange a regular tutorial time which should be protected from interruption in so far as possible; there should be indication that the student can seek additional help as needed but he should be encouraged to utilize the regular time for all but emergency matters.

(8) The importance of orientation; well-planned induction eases anxiety and gives the student the wherewithal to begin functioning.

(9) Draw the student into active participation early be getting him to say what he thinks he needs to know in order to get started. Keep up the practice of having the student formulate what he thinks he needs help with—what he needs to learn in order to carry out his responsibilities to clients.

(10) Hold the student to prompt recording, and utilize the recording as the basic teaching-learning tool in the supervisory discussions.

(11) Get the student started immediately in doing; do not delay in assigning cases or other appropriate projects.

(12) Keep the focus on the job to be done, giving recognition to feelings about the learning situation, but not losing track of responsibilities.

(13) Give the student the opportunity to develop his own professional 'style'; teach not by rote, but by principle, allowing the student to find his own ways of applying principles.

(14) Have enough courage to let the student learn; don't overprotect. With supervisory help the student can meet even very difficult demands without damage to the client.

11

HELPING STUDENTS IN FIELD PRACTICE IDENTIFY AND MODIFY BLOCKS TO LEARNING*

LOLA G. SELBY

THE social work student has to learn and learn rapidly, within his two brief years of graduate study, if he is to acquire even a beginning understanding of the principles, concepts, policies and processes that constitute the profession of social work. That the present two-year period of professional education provides the opportunity for no more than basic learning in the field is a generally accepted fact. Hence time is of the essence. For the educable student early identification of blocks to learning can speed the process of educational assimilation and professional development.

Imparting and acquiring social work learning is definitely complicated by the fact that social work education tests to the limit the integretive powers of the learner and the professional capacities of the educator. Social work education inevitably involves the student in a significant personal and emotional growth experience. As Hollis and Taylor point out, social work education makes four demands on the learner—in knowing, feeling, being and doing.[1] The social work student encountering these four demands must go through a process of personal reorganization in the development of his professional skills. As he begins to use himself in new ways in the helping and enabling role, as he develops increased self-awareness and understanding of others, and as he incorporates challenging new ideas from the curriculum, he experiences personal change through professional growth. Virginia Robinson refers to what occurs in this learning experience when she mentions 'the process of change, professionally initiated and limited', which becomes an organic growth process 'formed and directed by the unique nature of each individual self'.[2]

---

* Published in *The Social Service Review*, Vol. XXXIX, March 1955.
[1] See Ernest V. Hollis and Alice L. Taylor, *Social Work Education in the United States*, Columbia University Press, New York, 1951.
[2] Virginia P. Robinson, *The Dynamics of Supervision under Functional Controls*, University of Pennsylvania Press, Philadelphia, 1949, p. 137.

For the student at the graduate level impediments to learning are likely to be emotional rather than intellectual. Unless the student can permit himself to become personally and emotionally involved in the learning process, to the extent that his impulse to grow and change triumphs over his impulse to preserve his old ways of thinking and reacting, true learning cannot take place. Social work educators need to be fully aware of the emotional elements in learning—the doubts, uncertainties, fears and resistances that may impede the student's progress as well as the gratifications that may spur him on. It is essential that faculty members be ready to help the student deal with the blocks to his progress. This individualized help, however, must be focused on his professional development rather than on his personal needs and problems. If his personal difficulties are such that they lead him to seek in the school therapy rather than education, he should be encouraged to seek such help outside the school setting. The ultimate goal of his learning in classroom and field must always be kept in mind—self-assurance and independent functioning in the professional role and the ability to operate as a skilful and competent helper in the field of human relations without tripping over his own unconscious reactions, his personal value judgments, or his defences.

In the school curriculum there seem to be two areas that stimulate the most intense personal involvement on the part of the social work student, because these two areas implicitly demand direct use of self in a creative way. In field work and in the research project all the emotional elements of the student's learning come into play. The following discussion has to do with field work problems only.

To his surprise and/or dismay the student in field work may find himself using his characteristic defences in order to avoid facing performance demands, making necessary changes in self, or adapting himself to new experience. This already charged situation is intensified, no doubt, by the tutorial system of instruction always used in field work. As pointed out by Lucille Austin, the tutorial or supervisory method of teaching brings intensity of relationship into the foreground.[1] The relationship factor, plus the provocative content of social work course and field material naturally stimulates subjective reactions on the part of students. New insights about people and self, added to the supervisory relationship which tends to reactivate old authority-dependency conflicts or other basic conflicts, may impel use of defence

[1] Lucille N. Austin, 'Basic Principles of Supervision', *Social Casework*, XXXIII, December, 1952, pp. 411–18.

patterns for handling these conflicts, thereby inevitably arousing emotional response to the learning situation. The very newness of this kind of learning experience for the beginning student is in itself anxiety-provoking, calling for mobilization of old defences. The supervisor, or the faculty member serving in an advisory capacity to the student, has to recognize the student's demonstrated patterns of working and learning and help him become aware of those that hinder or interfere with his professional development. The sooner the supervisor can recognize the student's learning problems and his characteristic reactions to obstacles in learning, the sooner she can help him to cultivate new and more effective responses—to become more receptive to new ideas and new ways of functioning. The supervisor, of course, may use her discernment of a student's characteristic responses to help him in ways other than those utilizing direct interpretation.

Several questions arise in considering the foregoing postulations. Granted individual variation in response to new learning situations, how soon, in general, can a student's characteristic reactions to learning be recognized and his learning problems noted? How soon and in what way should they be brought to his attention? Who must define them—teacher or student? Who sets the learning pace—learner or mentor? Inasmuch as emotional factors are involved, where is the fine line of distinction between supervisory or educational counselling and therapy? What normative standards for evaluating educability and progress are appropriate in considering and dealing with students' learning patterns?

As has been indicated, because of the heavy personal demands that field work places on a student and because of the crucial nature of that particular learning experience, again and again the field work setting brings into focus with a clarity not so discernible elsewhere a student's characteristic reactions to learning. Subjective responses are less distilled in field work than in the classroom, where individual reactions are often modified by the academic environment to which the student has long since adapted himself. In field work the student finds it necessary to start using himself in a helping role at the same time that he is learning what he is supposed to be doing and what he should know in order to do it well. It is impossible to acquire field work experience by purely intellectual exercise, since use of the emotional as well as of the intellectual self is part of the process. Learning through field work may be a gratifying and maturing experience if the student is emotionally free to learn and does not have to spend his days erecting defences against change and self-understanding. On the other hand, if he is not free to learn, the student may have to spend much valuable time shadowboxing with his anxieties.

Blocks to learning, in the form of characteristic self-protective responses and ways of warding off change, show up early in field work. These blocks to learning may be spotted, with ample opportunity for confirmation, during the first semester of field work. The student absorbed in meeting the complex demands of his placement and in most instances not accustomed to thinking about or observing himself as a practitioner in action, is seldom aware at first of his defences against learning. The supervisor is the one who has to set up the structure within which the student may discover himself as he relates to his job requirements. Problems in learning may and should be discussed with the student when they appear and in the context of their appearance. The time for such discussion may be at any supervisory conference; the focus should always be on the student's job performance —what specifically seems to be assisting or impeding his progress at that given point in time. This does not mean that unrealistic demands are to be placed on the student for performance beyond his capacity and experience or that the supervisor holds up a mirror in which the student is forced to view his basic personality structure. Discussing problems in learning means rather that the student is helped to evaluate his day by day performance in the light of what his assignments demand of him, of how he goes about meeting the job requirements, and of how he feels about this activity. This discussion promotes the self-awareness that is so important in professional development. By the end of the first semester both beginning student and supervisor should be able together to formulate their thinking about the student's working and learning habits, along with those other aspects of his performance that become a part of his formal evaluation. The self-understanding achieved by the student in this process is a necessary step toward more conscious and effective use of himself during the next period of training. How much progress the student makes during the second semester in the knowing, feeling, doing and being aspects of his learning will depend in large part on how clearly he has already grasped 'how he characteristically uses himself and his knowledge, and what in his equipment needs development'.[1] This, in turn, hinges on his emotional readiness for self-awareness and on his capacity for change. If by the end of the second semester he has not been able to

[1] Frances T. Levinson, 'Principles and Practices in Supervision', in M. Robert Gomberg and Frances T. Levinson (eds.), *Diagnosis and Process in Family Counselling*, Family Service Association of America, New York, 1951, p. 151.

move ahead in working toward necessary change and development, it is to be anticipated that the school will question his readiness or capacity for second-year work.

The question of learning pace enters here, as well as the matter of educability for the profession of social work. Certainly much has yet to be discovered about how much maturation and integration can be expected of students within the two-year training period. These concerns have been thoughtfully discussed by Charlotte Towle.[1] While further study and more precise definition of normative standards are needed in the educational field, long experience in working with students has given social work educators some guideposts for recognizing what to expect of the student at given stages of his educational experience. Even though learning is definitely an individual matter, affected by individual capacity and emotional readiness, the school has to take the responsibility for determining what quality of performance shall be demanded of the student and what learning pace shall be considered standard. The field work instructor, in turn, has to take these norms into consideration at the same time that she recognizes individual differences in learning responses.

To make early identification of the student's learning problems, the supervisor must be able to foster the kind of relationship in which mutual trust and freedom of expression can prevail. She must be sure enough of her own function and role to accept responsibility for teaching and helping when her diagnostic abilities tell her what is happening to the student and what sort of help may be needed. Letting nature take its course in working through blocks to learning is not enough. A policy of watchful waiting is wasteful of both the student's and the supervisor's time. The sooner the student is helped to come to grips with his own learning problems, the sooner he will be able to begin to move ahead in the development of his professional capacities. This kind of self-discovery, within the context of learning how to become a social worker, may have therapeutic value for the student concerned, but it is basically an educational rather than a treatment experience. In the educational setting the student invests himself for the purpose of learning how to use himself in a professional capacity to help others. That he will grow personally as well as professionally during the process is inevitable, since the whole self is involved.

A few examples from supervisory practice with first-year students

[1] See Charlotte Towle, 'The Emotional Element in Learning in Professional Education for Social Work', in pamphlet entitled *Professional Education*, Five Papers Delivered at 29th Annual Meeting, American Association of Schools of Social Work, New York, March, 1948.

will make these points clear. Three type situations are here summarized, and supervisory method is sketched briefly to show how early identification of learning problems helped to resolve the difficulties and assisted in the student's professional development. The examples chosen illustrate only a few of the learning responses and problems out of many types that the supervisor may encounter in the teaching situation; but they depict how obstacles to goal-striving may affect some students and how the supervisor can help the student to work through them.

The student who clings to old standards.

The first type of learning reaction is noted in the student who at the beginning finds social work material and the requirements of field practice so anxiety-provoking and threatening that he must cope with the situation by clinging dogmatically to old standards and beliefs, closing the door to new experience and ideas. Such a student will be designated 'Student A'. He had come from a very religious and culturally circumscribed family background and had considered doing some kind of church-sponsored work before he chose to enter the profession of social work. Strongly motivated to 'help people' and to 'give service', Student A nevertheless found himself very fearful of and surprised at 'difference' in people who did not hold to his own standards. He was also made anxious by such social work concepts as ambivalence and 'growth comes from within', because he had been educated to follow certain well-defined precepts for thinking and behaviour and to view all ideas as falling into categories of black or white, acceptable or unacceptable. These reactions and anxieties came out early in the field work situation, affecting his work in the very first cases assigned to him. While on the one hand he was perturbed by the mores and behaviour of some of his clients, on the other hand he assumed that any attempt on his part to analyse why people felt and acted as they did was being 'judgmental'. The supervisor in case conference helped him to express his confusion by encouraging him to talk about what bothered him in each case situation. Student A brought up many of his own personal beliefs and pointed out how the clients seemed to differ from him in their sense of values; he also questioned what social work could do for them when they seemed to need so much more than material assistance. While the supervisor was accepting Student A's need at this point to measure all things by his personal standards and beliefs, nevertheless in the context of discussion of the student's work in specific cases the supervisor examined with him what was happening to make him so uncomfortable and confused. The feelings of 'difference' were not minimized but were recognized. Student A pondered all this and shortly came up with these questions: Did he have to give up his own ideas and standards if he became a social worker? Did he have to give up what for him seemed good? Here the supervisor frankly stated that some personal change was required of any student because learning meant growth and growth always involved change. This did not necessarily mean, however, that one always had to give up in one's own life what one had found to be philosophically sound for oneself. It meant, rather, that the student needed to understand the bases of his own beliefs and to attempt to understand other points of view. The supervisor commented that out of learning social work concepts and principles there might come more acceptance of one's own individuality, so that one was made less anxious by 'difference' in others. Student A pondered these comments and was able to relate them to an experience in the past when he had been challenged by some new ideas. As he realized that his conflicts were recognized but not condemned by the supervisor, he became less tense and began to permit himself some curiosity about what made his clients feel and behave as they did. By the end of the first semester Student A was able to verbalize, by specific reference to his own work, his problem in not having been able to accept behaviour he could not condone. He was also able to move beyond preoccupation with his own standards to consideration of his clients' needs and problems, individualizing them and attempting to understand what was involved in each situation. In the end-of-semester evaluation conference Student A commented that for the first time he was beginning to see how he had always reacted to new ideas or experience that put his old ideas and beliefs to the test—namely, that he tended to use all his energies in protective resistance. While he was still tempted sometimes to give up social work because it presented so disturbing a challenge, he now wanted to give himself more time to absorb the new ideas and experience. The supervisor herself thought that Student A had shown enough capacity for facing his conflicts, and was now sufficiently involved in the learning process, to make his continuation in school a feasible plan.

During the second semester Student A continued to test out his old attitudes and beliefs in the new learning situation. While 'acceptance' had been a hard-won concept for him, he began to be able to put it into practice. Increased understanding of personality growth and change gave him new insight into his own motivations as well as into the feelings and attitudes of his clients. He no longer fought 'difference' but was comfortable in individualizing his clients' needs and problems. He became absorbed in understanding and engaging in the helping process and only occasionally in supervisory conference indicated that he was still wrestling with some of his own problems. Towards the end of the second semester Student A told the supervisor that he now realized how much his initial negative reaction to social work concepts had been involved with his own growing-up process. He thought he had been unusually slow in effecting emancipation from parental and family ties (represented by his frantic clinging to old attitudes and ways of thinking), and he intended to talk this over with a therapist. The supervisor accepted these comments but made no attempt to explore with the student the bases of his conflicts. On his own initiative Student A followed through on his plan and arranged for some interviews with the psychiatrist at the student health centre. He did not discuss these with the supervisor in field work, but his work by the end of the year showed evidence of a sense of direction and personal security that had certainly been lacking in the beginning. Having faced some of his problems in incorporating new learning, Student A was, during the second year of his training, much less handicapped by them.

The student who fears responsibility.

A second type of learning problem is confronted by the beginning student who finds that social work training demands too much in the way of adult responsibility and who falls back on earlier dependency patterns in meeting new experience. Such a student will be designated 'Student B'. Young and limited in life-experience, Student B was outgoing, enthusiastic, eagerly looking forward to a career in what promised to be a very 'exciting' profession. Student B genuinely liked people and wanted to be liked in turn. A very attractive young person, she had always used her personality effectively in getting the response she wanted from others. The concepts of a professional approach and a professional self had little meaning for her. Student B almost immediately related to the supervisor as to a parent-figure, looking to her for advice, approval, and even the scheduling of her work. It was difficult for Student B to hold to regular conference times; she had always been able to confer with her mother whenever the spirit moved her. Student B also found it hard to hold herself to regular and consistent work habits and to take responsibility for her own learning.

During the first few weeks of field work the supervisor met this student's valid dependency needs but, as soon as the newness of the learning situation had worn off, began to hold her more strictly to account for her own job organization and required her to plan so that only emergencies had to be discussed outside the regular conference hours. The supervisor also held the conferences to discussion of the student's case material rather than the social chitchat that the student so beguilingly introduced. The student was at first surprised and then a little resistant to the idea that 'using her personality' with supervisor and clients was not enough. She had been rather proud of her ability to have such pleasant 'conversations' with her clients and she felt threatened by having to think of the interviews as more than that. She tried to explain away the superficiality of her approach by admitting charmingly that she should make more effort. The supervisor was sympathetic to the fact that learning in social work did take effort but continued to raise questions, case by case, that would require Student B to hold to the job structure and to thinking about what she was supposed to be doing in her work with clients. Frequently requested advice on what to do in specific instances was not given; instead, Student B was helped to acquire whatever resource material she needed in order to arrive at her own decisions as to a course of action. She was then encouraged to think analytically and objectively about the results of her activity. This was difficult. Student B wanted very much to please, but she had not been accustomed to taking responsibility without a blueprint to follow, and she was uneasy about risking her own ideas. The supervisor verbalized this 'diagnosis' in supervisory conference one day after the student had commented on the struggles she was having in writing a paper for the casework class. The student was able to take hold of this idea; she admitted feeling discouragement because she did not seem to be measuring up to the demands of social work training. For instance, she indicated, trying to write this paper had somehow made her see how much she was missing in her own work with clients. The supervisor said that Student B must be finding the responsibilities of field work very difficult and demanding. Student B agreed. In the next conference the student pursued this matter, verbalizing her dependency feelings and her conflicts over such feelings by saying that she 'felt like a baby' when it came to knowing what to do. She indicated also that never before had she found it necessary to exert so much self-discipline and effort to achieve. Now she realized that she could not depend on her personality alone; in social work she would have to learn to use her personality in a different way and for a different purpose. The supervisor indicated that Student B had a real asset in her pleasing personality if she really wanted to augment what she naturally possessed with professional understanding and self-discipline. Perhaps she needed to do some more thinking about her own motivation for choosing social work; perhaps she did not really want to invest the amount of effort required in social work training. Student B protested that she did want to become a social worker, and she knew that whether or not she achieved this goal was entirely up to her.

The second semester found Student B's work still uneven, but there was more evidence of her working toward change in herself. She also began to relate classroom material to field work learning in a more pertinent way and to apply in her own performance some of the insights gained from courses in casework and growth and change. Eventually she verbalized her concern over her dependency on authority figures such as teachers and the supervisor, because she began to realize how much more effort she had put into finding out what the teacher wanted and in seeking approval than she had put into thinking through her assignments independently. She linked this tendency to her pattern of relationship with her parents. The student was permitted to 'think out loud' about these things when she brought them up in supervisory conference, but whatever she verbalized was related to realities of her field work responsibilities and social work learning.

The supervisor did not force Student B's self-analysis but showed understanding and acceptance whenever she arrived at some new revelation in self-discovery. There were periods of regression when Student B blamed her learning difficulties on the supervisor with such complaints as 'You didn't explain enough' or 'Why did you allow me to continue my errors?' But gradually Student B began to gain more independence and self-reliance. By the end of the year, although still immature in many ways, she no longer tried to rationalize, project or explain away her mistakes or fumblings but in discussing her work could initiate evaluation of her own performance. A new seriousness of purpose and identification with professional demands was becoming apparent. Student B was trying very hard to grow up and to accept adult, professional responsibility. The supervisor no longer represented a mother-figure but came into focus as an instructor and consultant. By this time there seemed to be enough constructive self-involvement on the part of Student B, enough impetus to learn without spoon-feeding, to warrant acceptance of her application for admission to the second-year programme. During the following year Student B made further progress in acquiring personal and professional maturity.

The student who fears relationships.

Another type of learning reaction is typified by a third student, who, because of a basic lack of self-confidence, when facing new demands for use of self in social work training, needs to retreat for a while behind a wall of diffidence or to assume the role of observer rather than participant in the learning situation. This reaction is exemplified by 'Student C'.

Student C, with fine intellectual endowment, gave early demonstration in field work of analytical skill and sensitivity to clients' feelings. On the other hand, he showed marked hesitancy in relation to his own 'being and doing' in field practice. His observational powers and analytical gifts were indicated by his ability in recording to formulate what he saw in his case situations and what he thought was significant. At the same time, his own participation in interviews was halting, rather stilted, and reserved. He could not respond freely to others; too much risk of self was involved. Even with a strong sense of social responsibility and a sincere desire to help people, he nevertheless was blocked by his own self-consciousness and his feelings of ineptitude and inadequacy. Self-analytical and self-critical, he was somewhat aware of his problems, but fearful of revealing them or of asking for help. Student C met conscientiously all agency deadlines and job requirements to give his clients the service they needed, but his efforts to be helpful created in himself more anxiety than satisfaction. For some time he could not accept support or reassurance from the supervisor; as he struggled on alone, he became very self-depreciating because he was not measuring up to his own standards. Because of his quick perceptiveness and his ability to think conceptually, Student C's participation in supervisory conference was good when he could keep the focus off himself and in the area of intellectual discussion. When led into discussion of his own reactions or role in field work, he either froze up with uneasiness or took refuge in intellectualizing. He could express neither discomfort nor hostility. As time went on, he began to postpone seeing clients, rationalizing to himself that he needed to read and think more about what he was doing before he went into action.

The supervisor, recognizing Student C's basic lack of belief in himself and also his suspicion of controls or authority represented in supervision, attempted to be supportive and to help him voice some of his underlying feelings. In discussion of case material the supervisor took the initiative in verbalizing some of the student's reactions to his clients and some of his feelings of anxiety and uncertainty in the helping role. These feelings were treated as being quite understandable and acceptable. Job requirements were made as explicit and realistic as possible. When the student was self-depreciating, the realistic elements in the situation were separated from the unrealistic standards which the student tried to set up for himself. It was made clear that a mistake was not regarded as a mortal sin. Gradually Student C was able to come out of his shell occasionally to voice some of his real concerns about his work. An atmosphere of permissiveness and consistency and a holding to reality in discussion of job requirements eventually gave the student courage enough to express some negative feelings towards the demands of professional training and toward being supervised. As so often happens, the negatives were focused by the student on recording. Just why recording was irksome or painful for the student was discussed. The student himself recognized that what he felt to be unreasonable demands in meeting recording requirements had more to do with his own reactions to the learning situation than to anything else. He and the supervisor talked about how process recording meant putting one's self and one's professional activity on record. Student C said then that he had difficulty in responding to his clients' feelings and expressing interest in their problems, even though he wanted to do this. He wondered if he had what it took to relate to people spontaneously. Sometimes he was more concerned about the client's reactions to him than about his reactions to the client. These expressed feelings were accepted by the supervisor as being important but not devastating, and the student was helped to think out loud about his next interview—to anticipate what he needed to know in order to feel comfortable in conducting the interview.

A climax came early in the second semester when Student C was finally able to 'blow his top' in a supervisory conference after he was asked to revise some recording. The presenting problem was soon forgotten as he unloaded many of his frustrations, negative feelings and anxieties in connection with social work learning. He voiced his fear of close relationships, his fear of adverse reactions on the part of others, and his fear of handling emotion-laden material with clients. Again his feelings was given acceptance and recognized as problems in the way of his learning to work effectively with clients but also as problems confronting many other people trying to learn how to work in the field of human relations. The supervisor pointed out cases and specific interviews in which Student C had done well, indicating that the situation was far from hopeless. The student appeared to be relieved and expressed surprise that the school seemed to accept him despite his limitations. From this point on he began to develop more self-acceptance and hence was able to respond with less self-consciousness in the client-worker relationship. His ability to give and to respond appropriately in the helping role increased markedly, and by the end of the second semester he was no longer holding himself aloof but was fully participating in developing his professional skills, finding considerable personal as well as professional satisfaction in his new-found (though still admittedly precarious) acceptance of self.

Student C showed marked progress in the second year in his ability to establish meaningful relationships with clients and in arriving at a more realistic appraisal of his own strengths and limitations. He became less self-depreciating and more confident of his own abilities as a helping person.

Supervisors and faculty advisers will be able to recall from their own experience many other examples in which students' learning problems were seen and help was given to modify the difficulties. Consideration of these illustrations should serve to underscore the premise that there is need for early identification of patterns of response to learning obstacles and requirements, so that students may make use of their learning opportunities in a more conscious and productive way.

In summary it may be said that early identification of students' learning problems in social work education has important connotations both for the students and for the school assisting them in their professional development. Basic learning cannot take place unless a student is able to invest his whole self in the learning and growth process. Understanding how he reacts to new experience and to intellectual and emotional demands is a first step toward the student's modification of negative responses and resistance to change. Characteristic reactions to learning show up early in a student's career and come into focus with particular clarity in field work. There the relationship factor intensifies emotional response to learning. The supervisory role is fraught with peril if the supervisor is not clear in her understanding of her teaching and helping function. The supervisor is a logical candidate to become for the student a parental substitute or a symbol of authority-dependency conflict. Old emotional problems may be reactivated in this new situation. By helping the student to identify early his learning responses, the supervisor may control such transference elements and extricate herself from a wrongly conceived relationship. Helping the student to recognize the emotional aspects of learning is not therapy, although maturation and integration occur when the educable student is able to resolve some of his blocks to learning. Individual differences must be taken into account by social work educators in their teaching and helping methods, but the responsibility for determining what level of performance and what learning pace shall be considered standard for the student rests with the school. Both instructor and student are affected by these norms. The school is also responsible, through its individual instructors, for setting up the structure in class and field within which the student tests out his learning and discovers himself as he relates to professional discipline and learning requirements. Problems in learning may then be discussed in the context of their occurrence in a particular learning situation, and the focus may be kept on the use of self for professional purposes.

Attention given by social work educators to the emotional aspects of learning presupposes a firm administrative foundation, as represented by good admissions procedures and selection processes, and sound machinery for helping students withdraw if their learning problems prove to be too basic and deep-seated for modification in the social work training programme. It is obvious that close co-ordination between the school and its field placement agencies is necessary to ensure mutual understanding of educational requirements and goals and the proper channelling of student problems that have implications calling for administrative attention.

Finally, the educational approach of helping students to work through blocks to learning presupposes a closely integrated school curriculum and a continuity of experience for each student that will give him the opportunity for and, in fact, will require of him, personal and emotional as well as intellectual involvement in his learning. This does not discredit the 'breadth and character of graduate seminars' held up in the Hollis report as the *summun bonum* of professional education, nor does it imply, as the Hollis report fears, that field placements will be 'too largely focused on stimulating self-understanding or in counselling on how to improve service to clients', to the neglect of broader aspects of professional understanding.[1] On the contrary, the process of identifying students' learning problems in class and field and of working towards their modification gives recognition to the simple but potent fact that feelings and emotions operate in learning response and that this is particularly true where reorganization of self for professional performance is required.

[1] Hollis and Taylor, *op. cit.*, pp. 242 ff.

GEORGE ALLEN & UNWIN LTD

London: 40 Museum Street, W.C.1

Auckland: P.O. Box 36013, Northcote Central N.4
Barbados: P.O. Box 222, Bridgetown
Bombay: 15 Graham Road, Ballard Estate, Bombay 1
Buenos Aires: Escritorio 454-459, Florida 165
Beirut: Deeb Building, Jeanne d'Arc Street
Calcutta: 17 Chittaranjan Avenue, Calcutta 13
Cape Town: 68 Shortmarket Street
Hong Kong: 105 Wing On Mansion, 26 Hancow Road,
Kowloon
Ibadan: P.O. Box 62
Karachi: Karachi Chambers, McLeod Road
Madras: Mohan Mansions, 38c Mount Road, Madras 6
Mexico: Villalongin 32, Mexico 5, D.F.
Nairobi: P.O. Box 30583
New Delhi: 13-14 Asaf Ali Road, New Delhi 1
Ontario: 81 Curlew Drive, Don Mills
Philippines: P.O. Box 4322, Manila
Rio de Janeiro: Caixa Postal 2537-Zc-00
Singapore: 36c Prinsep Street, Singapore 7
Sydney, N.S.W.: Bradbury House, 55 York Street
Tokyo: P.O. Box 26, Kamata

Vol. 1   SOCIAL WORK WITH FAMILIES

This book gathers together some outstanding contributions to various aspects of social work with families. This subject is now more than ever of concern to social workers as fresh knowledge adds to their understanding of the dynamics of family life and interaction. The papers which compose this book are by well-known authors on both sides of the Atlantic. They are arranged in three sections, dealing with normal and less normal families as a group, with particular crisis situations for children, and with some more theoretical concepts contributing to an understanding of family types.

Vol. 2   NEW DEVELOPMENTS IN CASEWORK

This book gives examples of the most advanced thought about casework by well-known writers in England and the United States. The ground covered includes: the use of some current sociological theory in casework; analysis of the interpersonal relationships in casework; new thought about the appropriate use of authority with people whose own internal controls are weak and unreliable; recent advances in understanding and working with people who respond to action more easily than to words. These articles by well-known authorities illustrate the increased range of insight and skill required of modern caseworkers, and at the same time are highly readable, conveying complex ideas in language refreshingly free from jargon.

Vol. 3   SOCIAL WORK AND SOCIAL VALUES

This volume of the *Readings in Social Work* series will appeal especially to social workers, administrators, social work teachers and those who are becoming increasingly concerned about the whole question of value assumptions in social work. So far little has been written on a subject of lively discussion amongst practitioners and students alike; in this volume are gathered together some of the most influential and often quoted articles which have appeared in Britain and the United States in recent years. They deal not only with the general ethics of professional practice and specific situations but also with conflicting value judgments in administrative settings and the relation between administration and values.

1   SOCIAL WORK AND SOCIAL CHANGE

Eileen Younghusband

'... should be compulsory reading for students of social work and social administration of any age.'

Case Conference

'... covers the subject in a most instructive and useful manner and should be studied by all interested in the subject.'

Quarterly Review

5   PROFESSIONAL EDUCATION FOR
     SOCIAL WORK IN BRITAIN

Marjorie Smith

Professor Marjorie Smith's classic little book traces the story of professional education for social workers in this country, which has been a pioneer and has influenced countries overseas.

There were the various committees of the Charity Organization Society on training and social education and the contribution of such great figures as Lord Avebury, Alfred Marshall, Mrs Bosanquet, Sir Charles Loch and Professor Urwick. Professor Smith brings out the long-continued struggle to establish professional standards and genuine professional education through integrated training in both theory and practice. The book ends with some fascinating appendices, including an original paper by Alfred Marshall. It traces briefly but vividly the origin and gradual acceptance of the main principles on which social work and preparation for social work are now based.

'a standard work ... concise and illuminating ... lucid in style as in thought.'   *Times Educational Supplement*

'We are indebted to the author and the publishers for this study of a crucial period in the history of the development of professional social work in Britain. With immense clarity we are shown the long-drawn-out struggle to establish real professional social work education through courses of integrated study and practice.'

Social Work

13   MOTHER AND BABY HOMES

Jill Nicholson

There has recently been much discussion about the plight of the unmarried mother and her child; but very little of it has been based on fact. Mother and Baby Homes cater in fact for between 11,000 and 12,000 unmarried mothers each year, out of a total of 70,000; but there is hardly one generalization that would be applicable to all the Homes. Some are run by voluntary organizations, some by local authorities and some by religious groups. While some still retain the punitive attitude; others set themselves with much kindness to help the women — some of them mere schoolgirls, to face the difficulties of their position and to plan constructively for their own future and that of their babies. This book gives the facts but, even more, it gives the feelings and ideas of those most concerned — the mothers-to-be and those who care for them.

This is a careful and sensitive study. It is unique in putting on record for the first time the views of unmarried mothers themselves about the care they receive. Everybody who is concerned over the health and welfare of the unmarried mother in residential care should read this book.

LONDON: GEORGE ALLEN AND UNWIN LTD